Who's Crazy Now?

A family's story of tragedy, love, hope and perseverance

A doctor's quest to unlock a brain mystery

Danielle –
Blessings!
Let's keep lifting each other up!
Sue
Sept 16 2009

Who's Crazy Now?

Susan Rueb
Todd Clements, M.D.

Table of Contents

Foreword

A war is raging today among America's children and adults who are being misdiagnosed and treated for mental illness when the underlying condition is overlooked. Every day doctors prescribe medications without examining the organ that is being treated... the brain. These medications are aimed at controlling behavior but do little or nothing to bring healing. Some medications can ultimately be damaging to their physical health.

As you read this book, your heart will be touched by the struggle of Kristin Rueb and her loving parents, Susan and Jerry, who searched to find the answer to their daughter's troubling behavior. You will be impacted when you learn how they found Dr. Todd Clements, who is one of the few psychiatrists in the United States who is actually looking at how the brain functions in his patients. His diagnosis helped turn the tide on thirty years of misdirection and frustration.

As you read this true story, you will be moved to buy copies of this book and send them to your legislators and congressmen and women...write letters to your elected officials to help bring needed change to our health care system; so that Kristin's story is not repeated. *Who's Crazy Now?* is a must-read book for every parent, psychiatrist, psychologist, and pastor.

With respect,

Dr. Earl R. Henslin
Author of This is Your Brain on Joy
Founder of the Henslin Clinic, Brea, California

Who's Crazy Now?—Part 1
Susan Rueb

INTRODUCTION
Flashback... Who's Crazy Now?

As the plane hissed and lurched downward on the tarmac at LAX in Los Angeles carrying our daughter, Kristin, her self-inflicted cigarette burns were the least of her challenges as well as ours. Her younger brother, Jon took it on himself in June of 2001 to locate and bring his sister home to California from Vancouver, British Columbia. Though several attempts to rescue Kristin had been previously made, she remained in Vancouver existing on cocaine, heroin and a false sense of who she was. As her parents, we did not know where she was and had no contact with her for months. With a picture in his back pocket of Kristin and no clues to her whereabouts, Jon landed at the Vancouver Airport to look for his sister. Within two hours, he called us as he held Kristin tightly in his arms. He found her in a detox center with nothing but a hospital gown to her name. After a harrowing night with his sister still coming off her drug-induced paranoia, Jon carefully passed through airport security and immigration, bringing Kristin down to Southern California.

Each member of our family was on edge that summer day when the airplane touched down in L.A. Jon at 23 was already exhausted from the previous week's challenge when he stepped onto that plane with his 25 year old sister who was dazed, confused, angry and giddy. Kristin and Jon's thirteen year old sister, Jana, waited anxiously at home for the news of her sister's homecoming. My husband and I restlessly waited at the airport for our precious daughter but we were unprepared for who came walking off the plane that day. Kristin sauntered ahead of her brother with bandages covering her hands and parts of her face. Her thin, tired body tipped the scales at barely 100 pounds. Her 5′5″ athletic frame had disappeared into an emaciated, cocaine skeleton draped with tallow, translucent skin. Her once beautifully thick and shiny brunette hair now lay lifeless and twisted around her sad face. Our enthusiasm for the reunion quickly dissolved as we saw Jon walk behind her with a look of lost hope on his face shaking his head back and forth. Kristin acted like a frightened, vulnerable little animal as she drew back from us with a look of wonderment and desperation. I couldn't help but feel sorry for myself when I realized that my own daughter didn't seem to know who I was. This was the continuation of a journey of confusion and missteps that had deeply impacted every member of our family going back to Kristin's birth. Our experience could best be described like a baby's mobile hanging over a crib. When the center piece is jiggled, all of the rest of the pieces are moved as well. Kristin had unconsciously become the centerpiece of our family and we were all moving in different directions and at different speeds.

Chapter 1 Special Delivery

Santa Cruz, California August 3, 1975

I was both excited and scared on August 3, 1975. I was an elementary school teacher and on my way to the hospital to have my first baby. As the car raced toward my day with destiny, I thought to myself; I'm a teacher but I didn't teach babies. I had no real experience with babies. As a young girl I was not the babysitter type. In fact, I only remember babysitting for one lady…an exotic dancer at a motel in Portland, Oregon. My limited experience came when I was in high school and did not prepare me for giving birth to my own baby. Every first time mother is a little apprehensive when she is ready to give birth to her first child. Right? But, I was definitely not prepared for the dramatic childbirth that was planned for me. I started labor several times during my final weeks of pregnancy and had even been to the hospital only to have my labor stop.

This particular Sunday morning was our day. My husband Jerry, who was a youth pastor of a large church in Santa Cruz, California, was as thrilled as I was to coach me as I gave birth to our first child. I was rushed into the hospital, interviewed, questioned, probed and examined. When I finally got into the labor room and climbed into bed, the labor pains slowed down. The doctor came in. He ordered Pitocin to be given as an I.V. drip to "get me going and get our baby out to meet the world." After a few minutes the medication entered my bloodstream and, I felt the force of the first contraction. It came like a freight train hitting me head on. I quickly went into the Lamaze mode and began a breathing exercise that sounded like a boiling teapot running a marathon. After a ten minute contraction with no let up, Jerry turned to get up and call the doctor. I grabbed his shirt tightly and wouldn't let him go. As I spun out of control, I insisted that he stay with me and "help me breathe." Finally I got a break. One minute off and wham! The train was coming again and there was no stopping it. After a couple of hours and only three contractions, the doctor checked me for what he thought was a routine procedure. When he saw the desperation in both of our eyes he rushed over, swore and ripped the I.V. out of my arm. He yelled orders at the nursing staff making it very clear that there had been a mistake in the dosage of the Pitocin.

Quickly they attached monitors to track the beat of my heart and the baby's heart as well. I vividly remember medical staff scurrying and hurrying around my bedside and then I heard these words "She is in distress!" I thought to myself, "What an understatement!" The pain was horrific. I whined to Jerry, "I know that I can do this…I just can't do it today. Can we come back tomorrow?" But it was too late. That train had left the station and there was only one way out…forward to birth. The doctor faced a medical emergency because the baby was in fetal distress and I too was experiencing a medical crisis. After taking my vitals the doctor frowned and ordered another I.V. drip to slow things down. My searing pain started to ease and I wondered what the pain would have been like if that countermeasure had not slowed my contractions.

Soon I was wheeled into the cold and brightly-lit delivery room. I was near panic with pain and feeling overwhelmed by my lack of control. My body twitched and contracted until all I could do is beg for it to stop. Adding to the urgent situation was Kristin's position in the womb. She was upside down in the wrong position to make a proper entrance into the world. After attempting to manually turn the baby, the doctor ordered a nurse to give him the forceps. As he picked up the awkward medical instrument, I remember thinking it looked like a giant pair of salad tongs. With speed and force, the tongs went in grabbing my baby's head. With a couple of hard pulls Kristin was born. There was more scurrying and hurrying around and finally after a strategic "whack" on her bottom, my darling little baby began to cry...and cry she did! Crying was Kristin's first action and became her continuous behavior for most of her babyhood. Family members and friends assured me that those "little red marks on Kristin's head" left by the forceps would go away. Everyone reassured me that Kristin Louise Rueb was indeed beautiful. And, in fact, Kristin was beautiful. She had a precious little face, perfectly proportioned features, luxurious dark hair and flawless skin. The doctor declared her healthy and as he laid her across my tummy shaking like crazy, I cuddled her and ate a cheeseburger. Kristin cried.

Chapter 2 Cry Me a River

Santa Cruz, California August 3, 1975

I kept asking, "Is she alright? Why doesn't she stop crying?" The experienced mothers I knew all gave me the answer rookie mothers get. "You don't know anything about babies, do you?" Their patronizing answer seemed well deserved. I didn't know much about babies. However a growing uneasiness and a desperate hunt for clarity kept me searching for an answer to the growing question concerning my first child. After two weeks of non-stop crying I remember saying to the pediatrician, "Either give the baby some medicine, or give it to me." So at two weeks of age Kristin was given the powerful sedative Phenobarbital. Her little lips reached for the medicine via a tiny eye dropper. Kristin seemed to calm down but relief was brief.

I was told that babies get their days and nights mixed up. I wondered how long the upside-down schedule would go on. When she did sleep Kristin would sleep for hours and I was careful not to wake her. Some days she slept for 20 hours! During those quieter days my questions about her health seemed silly. What a perfect baby. She sleeps most of the time. However, when she woke up she screamed every waking hour and no matter what I did she would not be comforted out of her painful rage. I held her and tried to cuddle her but the more I tried, the more she jerked away and howled. Many trips to the doctor asking for help to calm my crying baby made me feel completely inadequate. Making matters worse, I was told that I was the one causing her to cry.

The doctor assumed that my overly-worried mothering was transferring an anxious feeling to her. He cited her trouble with breast feeding as an example. Kristin would only nurse on my right side and all of the coaxing that I could muster would not budge her. I gave into her odd infant nursing pattern and became engorged on one side and empty on the other. To keep from public embarrassment I went out with a pair of socks stuffed in my bra to balance my own look. Kristin seemed desperate to nurse, yet when she ate she pulled away and screamed as though she felt intense pain.

Every baby loves the rocking motion of a car so we put her in the car for a ride hoping to calm her. Instead of calming down, Kristin screamed louder. Car rides became a test of patience as she usually cried the entire time in the car. To help me cope, I was given the advice that toddlers needed to learn to play in a playpen. When I put Kristin inside the playpen loaded with toys she treated it more like a proverbial baby cage. Hoping that she would adjust, I left the room and tried to spy on her but she continued her screaming. When I went back into the room and took her from the playpen she was desperate and frightened. Determined, I tried the tough love approach and left her alone for well over an hour until she was sweaty and shaking. Finally I picked her up feeling like I had lost another battle of wills. Kristin just continued to cry in my arms.

Every mother longs to cuddle and hold her baby close. Kristin usually pulled away and screamed. This was confusing to me. Easy tasks and normal responses were a chore. Even the grocery store became a challenge. I had to make a grocery list from memory in the store aisles. I usually had about 15 minutes to get through the store without her screaming so loudly it caused shoppers to notice. I left a full grocery basket several times because of her persistent outbursts and loud tirades. I knew that something was very wrong but I had no idea what it was or where to turn. Trips to the doctor seemed to confirm that I was wrong and that Kristin was perfectly healthy. In some ways Kristin was developmentally ahead of other children. She was very verbal and spoke her first words before she was a year old. Her vocabulary was over 60 words at her first birthday. She had an amazing memory and would verbally repeat animal sounds and words found in her baby books.

By age two, Kristin was a handful. The terrible twos seemed to be named for her. We noticed her frustration when asked to wait for anything. My husband and I learned to set the timer on the stove to tell her when we were leaving for the park or the store. She would typically ask, "When are we going?" If the response was anything nebulous, like "in a little while," she would throw herself down and cry hysterically. If I accidentally dropped a pan in the kitchen the noise would cause her to tremble and scream. In an attempt to understand Kristin's outbursts I read books about the strong-willed child and behavior modification. Despite our sincerest efforts at parenting we couldn't seem to get concepts such as "no" "stop" or "come" across to her. Fatigued and puzzled by our dilemma, we sought the help and advice of a child psychologist well before her third birthday. Jerry and I, with our newborn son in arms, took little Kristin to the psychologist to get some guidance. We had little money to spend on counseling, but we were desperate for help. An hour later with less money in our wallet and no quick answers, we left the office confused, angry and feeling completely under confident. A creeping shame was added to the collection of unsavory feelings within our hearts. Standing at our living room window I watched as the school bus pulled away full of busy children talking and laughing. It was the first time in nineteen years that I wasn't either going to school or teaching school. My own private school at home with Kristin turned me into the student. Kristin was just beginning to teach me so much about myself and about who she really was. I held my little "teacher" in my arms that day. We both cried.

In my confusion I was beginning to feel like the whole world was out of order and I was the one out of sync. When other people found out about my struggle, I became the focal point of an avalanche of advice. Other young moms suggested using strategies that worked for them. However, nothing seemed to work in the mystifying communication process with little Kristin. Child psychologists at the time were writing on how to raise a strong-willed child. I read everything I could on how to communicate with and teach my strong-willed little toddler. Her wide vocabulary and intricate communication style told us that she understood, yet just wouldn't obey us. As time passed, anger and frustration began to fester within me. I was annoyed with Kristin's rebelliousness and I was irritated at anyone who did not understand what I was going through. I felt incompetent and helpless. No matter what method of parenting I chose, it seemed that nothing would "click" with Kristin. Why could she not understand acceptable behavior? Why did she choose to disregard my requests?

A simple act of getting out of the car became a painful drama that could ruin a sunny afternoon. In the days before car seats were required, we either held Kristin or allowed her to stand on the car seat between us. On one beautiful afternoon we were going out for lunch. Jerry stopped the car and I turned to Kristin offering her my arms to help her out of the car. She stubbornly pulled away from me and she found herself leaning into Jerry on the driver's side. He calmly stepped out and opened his arms to her to lift her down. Kristin immediately jerked back and defiantly stood in the middle of the front seat not knowing which way to go. She had a confused look on her face and didn't seem to know what to do. We both left our car doors open and said, "Come on, Kristin…let's go eat." She refused to move until we took a couple of steps toward the restaurant door. Then she climbed out and ran past us tripping on the curb. She fell down and skinned her knee but would not be comforted or reasoned with about the importance of coming or stopping when Mommy or Daddy called.

The safety issue became more crucial by the day because she would not obey nor did she seem to understand the connection between cause and effect. Kristin often repeated the same dangerous mistake more than a couple of times. She didn't remember her most painful lessons. More than once Kristin touched a hot iron and burned her little fingers. Regular burns on her fingers did not teach Kristin. Instead, I learned never to iron unless she was sleeping. She could not be taught not to touch. It occurred to me that I was being trained, not Kristin.

One evening at the dinner table when she was three years old, I asked her to pass the basket of bread to me. She didn't even look up. I raised my voice a little and asked one more time. No response. Then something registered within me that she was not hearing my voice. I lowered my volume to a whisper and covered my mouth asking her for the bread once again. She whined, cried and pulled my hand away saying, "Don't do that, Mommy." Then as she looked right at me I mouthed the same words without any sound at all. She smiled and said, "Here's the bread Mommy." We were shocked to discover that our little girl was reading lips. An examination by a hearing specialist revealed that Kristin's hearing was almost gone. The doctor's judgmental reprimand for not discerning her condition sooner caused me to feel incapable of parenting. Kristin had experienced perpetual ear infections from the time she was one month old which finally impaired her hearing. After the recommended surgery to correct Kristin's hearing, we thought she would overcome her seeming inability to obey a simple instruction. Tragically, this was not to be.

In addition to her other problems, Kristin was diagnosed with a "lazy eye." She wore her first pair of glasses before she turned two. With limited sight and hearing, the thought of carefully taking her glasses away at bedtime crushed my heart. As I put her to bed I remember the desperate look from her eyes. Later I realized that the feeling of being cut out or alone must have been intense for her. Try as hard as we might, we still could not seem to figure out what was hurting her. Once Kristin began to talk with fluency she didn't speak of hurt...she just behaved like she was hurting. She acted perplexed and we were baffled.

Most children experience times of being sick with coughs and colds. Kristin coughed constantly with bouts of ear infections and throat infections which exaggerated her coughing spells. I took Kristin to the pediatrician for her cough and though she coughed a bit in the office, the doctor didn't seem to think her condition was as severe as I described. When he doubted that Kristin coughed for hours about every 10 seconds, I pulled a small tape player out of my purse with a recording of the previous night's cacophony. Hearing the unbelievable, the doctor immediately ordered tests for allergies. So as Kristin entered into childhood, she faced life with hearing problems, glasses on her sweet face to correct poor vision, and twice-weekly injections for her allergies...all before 5 years of age! Kristin and I were both exhausted.

Chapter 3 School Daze

Santa Cruz, California 1980

Kristin could not wait to go to school and to fit into the school crowd. She was persistent and conscientious about planning what to wear, what school supplies should be purchased and even how she wanted me to fix her beautiful, brown hair. We took Kristin to Mar Vista Elementary school the weekend before it started so that she could navigate the building and know where the entrance to her classroom was on the first day. After about a week of driving Kristin to kindergarten she asked to ride the bus with the neighborhood kids. Our house was perfectly located. The bus stop was right outside our front door! Kristin walked out that first morning for her bus ride. As she reached the first step to board the bus, her little fingers gripped the step as she helped herself up. Soon a kindhearted 6th grade boy bent over to assist her. As she disappeared onto the coach, her one long pony tail braid down her back completed her sweet appearance. She looked as though she stepped out of a Norman Rockwell painting with her outfit of a navy blue corduroy jumper, a red sweater and red tights on her little legs. As the bus door breezed closed and swallowed up my firstborn, my heart leaped with the expectation that better days were ahead.

At the end of the school day I waited for Kristin to come home. I could hear the air breaks of the bus from our kitchen so I quickly walked out to meet Kristin. I wanted to hear about the adventures of kindergarten each day she came home. After riding the bus for about a week, the day came when the bus rounded the corner by our house, dropped into a lower gear, without stopping to unload and then sped on without dropping off Kristin. I ran after the bus in a panic, which did nothing except to tire me out. Back at the house I immediately called Jerry at his office and told him that Kristin did not get off of the school bus. We both sprang into action like any worried parent would do. I ran around the neighborhood thinking that Kristin had gotten mixed up and gotten off at the wrong stop. I looked everywhere. Jerry came home and combed the neighborhood looking everywhere for her. He then drove back down to Kristin's school and reported our missing daughter to her teacher. Perplexed at our missing child, the teacher assured him that she got on the bus to come home. We continued our frantic search desperate to find our child. Numerous trips through the neighborhood and phone calls to friends' houses did not reveal Kristin's whereabouts. An hour later the school bus drove up to our corner a second time that afternoon. We anxiously ran to the bus hoping for news of Kristin. A frazzled middle-aged female bus driver came down the stairs, rolled her eyes and motioned her hand for someone to exit her bus. There was a suspenseful pause. Then, dear little Kristin came bounding off the bus and down the stairs into our arms. We were thrilled to see her and yet confused over how she got there. The bus driver told us that as she pulled the bus into the school transit garage, she felt a hand on her shoulder and saw a bespectacled brown haired little girl facing her saying, "Hi." The startled bus driver said, "Oh my God." Kristin responded equally startled and said, "No, it's me, Kristin." The bus driver quickly drove back to the neighborhood and deposited her small inquisitive package. As the bus zoomed away, Kristin laughed and said that she hid in the back of the bus so that she could see where the bus went every day after she got off. We learned that day that Kristin had an incurable case of curiosity but without a healthy dose of fear.

As she grew, Kristin tried to explore her world. Her inability to understand the world around her created few dull moments at the Rueb household. Parenting a child with a personality that is constantly swimming upstream against the norm was at times exasperating. I desperately wanted to love, protect, honor and teach the child that God had chosen to give to me. I swung from consistent discipline to an open and loose parenting style, both resulting in the same stonewalling behavior of Kristin. If we asked her to come, she ran. When we took her hand, she pulled away. My closest moments with my little one were when I had her in my lap in the rocking chair reading stories to her. This was something that I happily started the day we brought her home from the hospital. It was a shock when at five months she began to make animal sounds, mimicking me out of the baby book. The obvious intelligence of our child made us all the more confused about her behavior. Our inability to teach her the appropriate behavior and to learn the consequences of her actions seemed to put the spotlight on our failure as parents. Many times I cried out in frustration, questioning God about this beautiful child that He gave to us. I kept thinking that God would not give us more than we could handle nor would He hide His solutions from us. Jerry tried to reassure me that we needed only to continue to do all that we knew to be right...even if our actions did not produce immediate results. I wanted to believe my husband's advice because I wanted a brighter future for Kristin. But when she did not change I found it to be a difficult pill to swallow.

Self help books, magazines and professional articles in the child psychology arena only worked to confuse me and set me up for more feelings of failure. As a young pastor's wife, even the Bible confused me. I had been raised in a Christian home with parents who loved and trusted God to reveal the blue print for their lives. Faith in the middle of adversity was not a stranger to my childhood. My own parents experienced a difficult marital separation following the death of their firstborn. Later they were miraculously reunited and started a family. My brother was born and then I came five years later. My birth risked my mother's life. Her doctor advised her to seek an abortion but she trusted God for the outcome. Then my father became blind as a result of an unusual circumstance when I was a year old. I was raised to believe that faith and optimism amid hardship is the norm. Yet for me, a darling little brown-haired girl who appeared to be strong-willed and stubbornly obstinate to her parents was rewriting the book. I grew up with difficult circumstances and I had learned to trust God for my life. Coming from such a strong Christian background, it became difficult to bear the burden of not being able to adequately handle the raising of our first child. My own Christian faith began to teeter as I questioned God and His wisdom of not giving me what I needed to cope and lovingly care for Kristin.

Just before Kristin entered the first grade, our family moved from California to Vancouver, British Columbia in 1981. On her first day of school in Canada, Kristin let loose of my hand in the gymnasium and confidently walked toward her classmates who were grouped to go off with their new leader and mentor, their first grade teacher. The feeling in the pit of my stomach was not unlike most mothers sending their first child off to school, however I had reason to believe that my feeling was different from other moms. Like a child's puzzle, there was a giant piece of information that was missing when it came to Kristin, but I didn't know what it was. For six years I exhausted the learning and wisdom gained from being an elementary school teacher, the wife of a good man and the daughter of courageous parents. Still I could not unlock the mystery of my firstborn. Now it was time to hand over my enigmatic child to someone who I was hoping would know more about my daughter than I had figured out. Maybe this was just what Kristin needed. Perhaps I was the problem, not Kristin. Maybe my feelings of being an inadequate parent were justified.

In my desire to connect the dots I reasoned that it was Kristin's time to become more independent, to learn, to cope, to work together with peers and to begin her journey of carving out her life's purpose and passion. This was the normal, natural passage of life. I was thrilled for her to grow and to develop successful relationships and achieve her dreams. My feelings of excitement for Kristin were mixed with feelings of confusion and apprehension. Though I rarely verbalized those feelings of mysterious fear, those assumptions and feelings were validated when other parents deliberately told me what I was doing wrong. In spite of all these cascading feelings there was a place deep inside of me that told me something was not right with Kristin. I just couldn't put my finger on what it was. Kristin looked like a darling little girl with a turned up nose, a mischievous grin and a vocabulary that was astounding.

As it turned out, school was tough for Kristin.

She needed to work especially hard to satisfy what was required of her. There was often a troubled blank look out of her eyes when either Jerry or I would attempt to explain a school homework assignment or concept. Looking back on school pictures, it is evident that sadness was bleeding through the carefully choreographed, photographic smile. Kristin did not have the child-like spontaneous joy that first graders usually have. The running, skipping, laughing and silliness were not common place for Kristin. One of her early teachers remembers Kristin as being a serious little soul with some very grown up ideas stuck in her mind. Without any prompting Kristin told a little friend of hers that she didn't worry about getting hit by a car, because she knew she would go to heaven. Her thought patterns and behavior were strange but she didn't have obvious symptoms like some of her classmates who took medication. Nor did Kristin require special classes or extra care to coach her academically. With extra parental help with homework, she fell in the low normal part of the scale of school children academically.

Third grade became a pivotal point in time for Kristin. Her teacher was more than ready to retire and had taught her third grade pupils successfully for many years. Kristin became the proverbial rock in her teacher's shoe. Though Kristin tried to please, it seemed that she just could not satisfy her teacher nor was her teacher remotely thrilled with Kristin. One rainy Friday afternoon, I went inside the school looking for Kristin because she didn't come out with the other students at the end of the school day. I ran into the school dodging the rain puddles and rounded the corner, stopping at Kristin's classroom door. Mrs. Boggs was sitting at her desk and Kristin was standing at her side looking up to her through her glasses, appearing like a scared little rabbit wanting to escape. Mrs. Boggs was drilling Kristin in the various values of coins using staccato-like language at breakneck speed with questions like, "How many pennies in a nickel?" "How many nickels in a dime?" "How many dimes in a dollar?" "How many nickels are in a quarter?" I watched as Kristin appeared to be shaken and dazed. The faster Mrs. Boggs talked and shuffled the coins around on her desk, the more confused and frightened Kristin became. I must have startled both Kristin and Mrs. Boggs as I stormed in resembling an angry Little Red Riding Hood in my red raincoat. In that moment my life seemed to be falling apart. My son, Jon was waiting for me in the car, I was in the middle of a miscarriage and my little third grader was being interrogated like a juvenile delinquent. With my hormones in a state of disastrous disarray, I unloaded my verbal ammunition aiming it right at the teacher.

The injustice I felt over Kristin's mistreatment was overwhelming. Kristin had not been given the chance to participate in art the week before because she didn't bring a bag full of seeds for her art project. I discovered that for an entire week the class was told "not to be like Kristin who forgot her seeds and had to do math." Her classmates gave me the painful information that Kristin was been singled out and embarrassed at school. I watched Kristin's lip tremble with fear as I lit into the elementary school teacher with all of these accusations. When I asked what was going on, the teacher told me she found it difficult to believe that any child growing up in this affluent community wouldn't know money denominations and she thought that Kristin was just being stubborn. I let her know that I had expected her to teach my child the three R's but that up until this time in her life, her father and I took care of her financial obligations. I did not want Kristin harmed with such aggressive scrutiny. My anger reached a boiling point when I was told that this teacher had put Kristin in a dark closet alone to figure out her math questions when the rest of the class was doing the art project.

Other episodes at school concerned me about this teacher too. There was the mistaken identity of another little girl who wore glasses like Kristin who violated the school rules by coming into the building during lunch time. Teachers pressured Kristin about the incident, she finally confessed to the infraction. Kristin confessed to get the teacher off of her case despite the fact that it was another girl who had broken the rules. When I was through with my tirade, I looked over at Kristin expecting her to see me as her champion and I watched as she began to cry hopelessly. The harsh conversation was just too much for Kristin. I believe we both lost that day. Kristin lost a new sense of who she was and I lost my grasp on what disturbed Kristin. As time went on, Kristin's reputation at school became jaded and disrupted. She withdrew and retreated inside of herself becoming a sad little girl. Her sadness only escalated our confusion with feelings of frustration and fear.

By the sixth grade, though there were a few friends from church and the neighborhood, Kristin felt separated from her peers. She told me that she "felt different" than the other kids at school. At the time, I thought that with puberty's onset, we should be poised like other parents to deal with the drama of being a pre-teenager. As Kristin developed into adolescence there was always a measure of secrecy about her. She seemed to hide the very essence of who she was, especially around the house. We were prepared for the normal collisions that appear with youth and their parents. Oddly, at first she seemed particularly interested in pleasing us and fitting in with her world.

After three miscarriages and one particularly difficult labor and delivery of a dead baby, my broken heart was coming alive again when Kristin's baby sister, Jana, was born in 1987. Kristin was 12. I remember joyfully laughing and saying that I was the only woman in the neighborhood with one child using diapers and another one using tampons. Kristin loved her baby sister and enjoyed the busy household that a new baby brings. I even thought that this new addition to our family would help to lift the dark sadness that Kristin had. And really, I believe it did...for awhile.

One day after school in Junior High, Kristin politely asked Jerry and me to accompany her into the living room. She had something that she wanted to tell us. We sat down and she faced us with, "I want you to help me lose some weight. I don't like the way I look and I want to change that." She mentioned how that some boy at school told her she had "a fat rear end" and called her a name. We thought she was cute for how she asked for the help and for her deliberate way of talking to us. We thought she was the normal teen who is never satisfied with their looks and just wanted to get in shape. Kristin's response was to run, diet and pay close attention to her weight. There were winter evenings in Vancouver when I waited to serve dinner because Kristin was still out running. More than a few times she would come in drenched and aching from the run. She could run and run and run and even caused her Dad to think twice before consenting to run with her because of her grueling daily journeys. After an injury that caused her some pain, she would not think of stopping. Kristin seemed obsessed. I asked her, "If you begin to hurt while you are running, you stop don't you?" Kristin looked confused. "Oh no, Mom...I don't stop until I get to the end." The pain was no deterrent to her. Her strong will continued to keep her going whether it was exercise, school work or an argument. It was as though she had tunnel vision and an over-developed sense of completion. Or was she just stuck?

One Saturday afternoon our family was whisked out of the house to allow a real estate person to show our home, which was up for sale. When we all came back into the pristine house I found vomit in the upstairs bathroom. I was furious that a potential buyer would vomit and leave it without flushing. Everyone agreed. It became apparent not long after, that it belonged to Kristin. She was dealing with bulimia. Kristin's new problem meant more books read, conversations, late night chats and even trips to a psychiatrist. But nothing alleviated Kristin's eating disorder. Kristin continued to be the mystery whom we dearly loved. Meanwhile, she felt emotionally separated from us because we lacked the ability to understand her. The storm had been brewing for years, and it was about to erupt.

Chapter 4 Sign Posts to a Dead End

Vancouver, B.C. 1990

Living in a small community in British Columbia had its advantages. People knew each other. There were few strangers in the town and there was the close knit family feel throughout the four mile square suburban bedroom community south of Vancouver. Being a member of a pastor's family in a small community in British Columbia had its disadvantages. Though we made great efforts to create a normal family life in the community at large and in our church congregation, our children couldn't help but feel the social pressure of being the "preacher's kids." Not much was apt to go unnoticed within the boundaries of our town. It was a like living in a place that was a cross between the village of Mitford and the Fox News Channel. Episodes of our family lore spun around the community. A speeding ticket, a car accident, driving back from Vancouver in a bathrobe, tying a chicken on the hood of our car through the Canadian border were all definitely noticed, chuckled at and understood. These were situations that Jerry and I acknowledged and owned because we embraced life with all it brings.

Maturity gives resource to cope with surprises. As young parents we were in control of the circumstances. I always thought that life was far too serious and needed to be laughed at more often. My philosophy was—life happens and why not take some joy in it? With Kristin's problems growing by the day a big question loomed on the horizon. How would I do when I could not be in control? What would my response be when the surprises were not fun and when they involved Kristin and how she related to others in the community? I began to feel the noose of public scrutiny tighten around my neck one clear fall afternoon when I was called to the local drug store and was told to come and "pick up your daughter." I snapped the baby in the car seat and rushed down to the store. Kristin was seated in a back room with a policeman looking tired, disgusted and sad. I couldn't believe my ears. "What? She stole some lipstick?" Was he kidding me? I considered myself the lipstick queen with at least 20 lipsticks in my purse at one time. If Kristin wanted a lipstick I would have given her one of mine. The security officer told Kristin that she couldn't come back into the store until she was 18 years old. She had been caught by the in house security cameras and taken into the office. Her girlfriend who was with her did not even see the incident and did not know where Kristin had gone. After my brief and embarrassing conversation with the officer, I drove Kristin home. We sat in the car and I tried my best to be stern yet calm in my approach. Immediately, my memory flashed back to stealing something from a store when I was in Junior High. This type of situation was not out of the normal range for teenagers, so I took the opportunity to thoroughly explain the consequences of such actions. With Kristin listening intently, I methodically covered the result of not being able to shop there for years, needing to call her friend to truthfully explain what happened and why she had "disappeared," and the dire consequences if a habit of such things formed...one goes to jail. She looked at me tearfully and shook her head in agreement and was so sorry, promising never to do such a thing again. I couldn't help but notice a vague confusion in her eyes that day. I chalked it up to a learning experience and one that parents of teenagers go through regularly. But did Kristin really understand me? The incident was over and put aside to be forgotten. Little did I know that it was the first step of more to come.

Kristin worked at her first job after school doing office cleaning at a local financial company. My face went hot and my stomach dropped when I got a phone call from one of the employees who was also a church member. The staff suspected Kristin of stealing money from various employees. So they planted some money in a particular place and caught Kristin in the act. I was devastated. I was shocked, sickened and extremely sad. She was terminated on October 31st which became a Halloween night that was most certainly dark and ghoulish for us as we tried to contemplate what had happened.

Later that same year our family was invited to Christmas dinner at some friends' house. It felt so good to come into a warm and welcoming home during the holidays and be treated to a delicious meal along with fun and bright conversations. We went home that night tired but filled with the satisfaction of a lovely evening with friends. A couple of days later I got a call from the hostess that hit me like a kick in the stomach. She suspected that Kristin had taken her daughter's pearl earrings. I reeled with hurt as I listened to what was an all too dark and confusing phone call. The conversation turned odd when my friend suggested that there might be something mentally wrong with Kristin. How could she? How dare she say that? Our daughter is not crazy. She is difficult. She is confused. She is a mystery and she has behavior challenges, but she is not mental. We confronted Kristin about the earrings and after lying, she finally admitted to taking them. We couldn't get beyond the action to the motivation. Our questions of "Why?" were never answered. Like any responsible parent wanting to teach their child morals, Jerry took her to face the family and to apologize. This was becoming all too commonplace since it was done at the work place as was done at the drug store. Kristin's behavior was beginning to feel like a pattern that did not fit well into a good family like ours. I wish I could say it never happened again, but that would not be true. A constant undercurrent of apprehension filled our home as we hoped that Kristin was on a better road but invariably the phone would ring with another set of bad news. We spent sleepless nights worrying, praying and discussing what to do with such a wayward and delinquent child. The busyness of a pastor's schedule, my elementary substitute teaching and caring for two other children made us ripe for overload and confusion about what to do.

Late one night after coming back with Kristin from a ladies' church event, I walked into the family room as Kristin was just coming in the back sliding door. I could see her clearly as she put out a cigarette. I couldn't believe my eyes. I was stunned. "Kristin, you don't smoke!" I said. What followed was a very enlightening conversation that brought me up to speed on my daughter's lifestyle. Other upsetting clues began to emerge. Like the night when I overheard her and a few girlfriends in the hot tub swearing like a submarine full of sailors. Her language was coarse, harsh and sounded like she was a completely different person than the Kristin I knew.

A mother's instincts kick in when they suspect their children are in trouble. I had this feeling that she abused alcohol. My husband tried to quiet my fears saying that I was becoming too intense in scrutinizing Kristin's behavior. We were non-drinkers and had no alcohol in the house. At the time my accusation seemed outrageous. Our son Jon jumped into the mix defending Kristin saying that both he and Kristin needed a mom and not an investigator. I was taken aback by his words because I so wanted to be just that....a mom who loved and cared for her children. I wanted to be a mom who both loved and yet was firm. And, most of all, I wanted to be loved for being that way. Perhaps that is why I was so shaken when I found a fifth of tequila on our china cabinet shelf reserved for English tea cups. It was like watching a beautiful picture being defaced.

Chapter 5 The Avalanche

Vancouver, B.C. 1995

I had a war going on inside of me. How do we address Kristin's behavior? Are we being too tight and conservative to allow our children to grow and make mistakes that have consequences? Are we willing to give them space to learn? The dots that defined Kristin's behavior were getting closer together making a composite picture that portrayed Kristin as a girl in deep trouble. At this point even my faith was shaken. I believed God would help me through any and all circumstances of my life. I watched carefully how my parents worked through their difficult situations and how God showed up to do miracles in their lives. Yet with Kristin something was different. We tried every avenue that we could think of and it seemed we always ended up on a dead-end road with road kill all around us. Counselors, teachers, friends, psychologists, Christian leaders and family members all were baffled. What was the missing piece that would bring peace to Kristin and our family?

I've never been in an avalanche; however I've read that it is extremely quiet just before the tumultuous event. That was how we felt the year that Kristin went off to a Christian university in southern California. Jerry was on the board of the University so he was able to get concessions for Kristin to be accepted. And there was some financial help offered, so we sent her there. We were more excited to go than she was. We had numerous personal contacts with people in the area that gave us a false sense of security. A counseling center on campus set Kristin up with appointments for regular help. She stood at the airport looking calm and appearing confident. Yet underneath she was apprehensive because of the new challenge that lay before her in college. With few boundaries and almost boundless independence Kristin was on a path toward destruction. With little ability to make clear and positive decisions, it wasn't long and we knew she would not make it there.

Kristin worked in a coffee shop near the campus and hooked up with some students who were less than serious about school. Those friends introduced her to illegal drugs and the avalanche began. She struggled for emotional balance and academic success but lost both battles. The university put her on academic leave and she came home that summer a year older and a year wiser in the ways of survival. Soon she fell back into familiar patterns of stealing, lying, smoking, swearing and using illegal drugs to cope with her feelings of being out of control. Unable to return to college, she lived at home with us trying to sift through her issues. After making some hasty promises about keeping herself free from trouble, we helped her get set up in an apartment. Things looked more normal when she landed a job. We mistakenly believed that she was progressing and getting free of her challenges. Unfortunately, her life was beginning to be a wild rollercoaster ride with constant and unexpected ups and downs.

As Kristin's path to destruction gathered speed many people would tilt their head down and peer at us, expressing their sadness and sorrow over a child gone wild. We learned that some people do not know what to say or how to truly give understanding or comfort when they see a family in crisis. But several others did come along side of us to care for us and for

Kristin just as we were. To our surprise we had friends who were the victims of Kristin's misbehavior who continued to love and care for us and for her. But in spite of all our hoping for the best and support from friends, Kristin's avalanche was speeding up. Every time a new catastrophe would cascade into our lives I began to think we were getting closer to the end. Well-meaning people would tell me that she just needed to "hit bottom" and then she could begin to heal and repair. I believed them and strapped on my seat belt for the ride of my life.

An avalanche is a rapid downhill flow of a large mass of snow and ice dislodged from a mountainside. We were witnessing the effects of the avalanche in Kristin's life; however we still did not know what was at the base. As devoted parents we questioned what our part was in the collision. Money, time, thought, prayer, soul searching and other resources were exhausted to come up with the answer. We knew that our parenting was imperfect and we also knew that we loved our children deeply. So why was Kristin so troubled coming from a loving home? Life does not guarantee fairness or all the answers to our questions. When we face dark moments even faith in God does not immediately yield answers. The more we didn't know, the more we were determined to patiently wait on God for what He was doing.

Meanwhile, watching Kristin leave the house and not knowing exactly where she was going or when she would return was painful. Many times over the next months Jerry went downtown and just drove around looking for our disorientated daughter. Once he stopped at a light on the east side of Vancouver and waited for the pedestrians to cross while the rain hit the front window. In a state of desperation, he looked up to see the girl crossing the street was our dear Kristin. He leaned over and opened the passenger door and she got in. After a long and loving talk from Jerry, Kristin said, "Thanks, Dad." and got out. We didn't see her for days. There was no connection between what we were saying to her and how she responded. She was experiencing life in how she chose to live.

One redeeming fact kept us from completely falling apart. Love was clearly communicated throughout the entire nightmare of Kristin's journey. No matter how confused she became, she remained clear on the fact of our love for her and hers for us. But we were living in the middle of a terrifying dream. On the worst of days we wondered how we could keep going on with everyday life. Would life ever be normal again when a family has a child who had turned her back on her family values and common sense to exchange it for a dark life of drugs and alcohol? We honestly did not know. In our fog there was something that kept propelling us forward. We could not make peace with the idea that it would always be this way. Though tempted, we did not give up on God and His mysterious ways. Thankfully, He certainly did not give up on us.

One chilly November evening Jerry came to a personal and professional roadblock. Feeling defeated and discouraged he called a friend and mentor in Colorado. Dr. Vernon Grounds was president of the graduate school where Jerry got his theological degree. Jerry bared his soul to his wise mentor, asking him if it was time to quit the ministry that God had called him to so many years before. With calm assurance Dr. Grounds listened and then pointed Jerry to read Isaiah chapter one where God laments over His rebellious children. "Hear, O heavens! Listen, O earth! For the LORD has spoken: "I reared children and brought them up, but they have rebelled against me." Isaiah 1:2 The Scripture leaped off the page. Dr. Grounds interpreted it this way. If God who is a perfect father had children who rebelled against Him, what makes anyone think that an imperfect human father wouldn't have children rebel again him? The wise mentor's counsel was; "How are you managing the situation? She is old enough to make her own decisions. She is an adult child." Staying in the ministry did not require a man to be perfect but it did call him to be patient and forgiving. It was a time of real introspection for both of us.

Kristin was now in her twenties, not living with us and indulging in a destructive lifestyle. I cringed when I read the newspapers or listened to the news on television. Would our daughter be the next headline? But the never-ending question kept creeping into my mind, "What is the key to unlock Kristin's compulsion to self destruction?" We could not figure it out, so it was time to seek more professional help. When a staff member at church suggested that Kristin needed residential rehabilitation for her drug habit, it was difficult to grasp. I had heard about denial and hiding from one's personal problems and yet I just couldn't seem to believe that our daughter could have such a deep problem. She grew up in a close knit family with values, love, care and accountability. Even after going through a litany of situations that pointed to addiction, it was nearly impossible to think Kristin was actually dependent on drugs. Like most people I had read books, watched Oprah, listened to talk radio and heard parent after parent speak about their own inability to face the fact of the child's addiction. Had I become a denying parent? I defined myself as being a person who is never afraid to confront an issue. We dealt firmly and consistently with all of our children. We acknowledged Kristin's repentant behavior and we willingly consulted others to learn how to cope. But was she was getting better or was she really addicted?

Drug addiction is a strange and insidious condition. It negatively affects the user and those around the user. Even the most vigilant parents can be swept into a co-dependency or a cloudy denial. Jerry and I were dramatically affected. We knew we couldn't just stand by and watch Kristin destroy herself, so we made a clear decision to get the help she needed. This decision began the long expedition to fix Kristin. At first our sincere desire to help find a cure for Kristin played into her failure to receive that help. We desperately wanted to help her and she desperately wanted to please us. I recall carrying her suitcase for her as we walked into the Salvation Army Rehab Center in Vancouver one afternoon. If I closed my eyes tightly, I could nearly think it was camp or a college and not a rehab center. The loud slam of the door and the immediate lockdown shook away my fleeting fantasy. Kristin obediently and deliberately went into the center firmly believing that this was going to be the beginning of the end of her challenges. I believed that as well. After a tearful goodbye and Kristin reassuring me that she was going to do well, I left the center and cried all the way home. Over the several weeks that she was there our entire family made regular visits to encourage her. We were all present on the day she "graduated" from the program. Our family walked out of the center together sensing hope for the future. Jon and Jana hugging Kristin offering her their congratulations remains a beautiful picture in my mind to this very day. I couldn't have known that day just how far we still had to go. It is sort of like moving day. Just when you think you are about done packing, you are usually about half way done. Drug addiction is merely not a problem to be solved, but an enemy to be reckoned with for a long time. We were all learning more than we wanted to learn.

It wasn't long after she came home from the rehab center that Kristin was offered a job downtown working as a receptionist. We were happy with her for the chance at a new life without drugs. We were on the right path once again. Not long into her job I was awakened late at night at the front door to see Kristin being held up by a young man whom I'd never met. Her speech was slurred, her eyes wild, and she jerked violently and yet she was strangely compliant with her escort. Something was terribly wrong. We steered Kristin in the den and sat her on the couch. The guy seemed anxious and told us that she was high on cocaine and he wished that he had a marijuana joint to give her to calm her down. I reached into my robe pocket and pulled out something that I'd found on the ground outside earlier and that I'd meant to show Jerry. The guy looked delighted. "Thanks, this will help her." What was I doing? I was finding joints on the sidewalk and giving them to my daughter? What was happening? Was **I** crazy?

This event became the beginning of an obsessive period of time in our family's life. Kristin was obsessive about finding the next satisfying hit of street drugs and we were obsessed with tracking down Kristin and sorting out the behavior that was defining her. Like a river at flood stage, Kristin and everything about her began to completely take over our family. The tension in the house grew thick. The conversations were long and arduous among a few members and very short and politely focused with others. War is always a last resort because war is hell as any experienced soldier will testify. But war is an action that must be entered into when it is an absolute necessity. We had a war on our hands. One thing became very clear to us. In order to fight this war we needed to have a clear fix on who the enemy was in Kristin's war. The war on drugs became more than a political slogan to us. Unlike many bureaucrats, we were fighting this war face-to-face with the enemy. We learned that the enemy uses its victims to do the deadly work of distribution. Governments spend great amounts of time, money and energy to wipe out the use of drugs, but it is usually spent on the wrong people. How does one fight the enemy of drugs and yet help the individual who is addicted to the enemy? This became our immediate challenge. I found my way into the ranks of parents who had children on drugs. I attended round table meetings with strangers, yet I felt a close kinship to them because of our common challenge of drugs and alcohol. Both Jerry and I gave our first names many times at Alcohol and Narcotics Anonymous meetings with and without Kristin to get the help we so desperately needed. Kristin went through a series of residential drug treatment programs and was eventually released either because she had finished the program or she had broken the rules and was asked to leave. Rules were a constant problem for Kristin to obey. Smoking inside, coming in on time and not taking others' belongings were consistently ignored.

The rollercoaster of our life with Kristin sped up and kept rolling at the lower levels of existence. We continued to seek help but Kristin's habit was increasing and eating her alive. The low point came one dark, rainy night in East Vancouver. I had taken my turn to look for Kristin with a friend of ours who was a Vancouver policeman. Jerry and I had searched for days and this particular night, I couldn't stand the thought of remaining safe and warm at home when our daughter was lost in the city. As we quietly and carefully slid through the dark parts of the warehouse -lined streets of Vancouver, our friend stopped the car and put down the electric window on his side. There in the night, I could see many women, young and old standing around talking, laughing, pulling their coats or sweaters around themselves. It was like disturbing a flock of crows. As the car stopped, the group scattered. Then one of them called out to her associates, "It's okay; it's just the mom." Instantly, many of the girls came over to the car and I began to talk with them. I asked them about their families, where they came from and how they got to this place. My heart was heavy and burdened for them and their faces seemed to call out in distress to me. Yet, when I offered any kind of real assistance, they turned and walked away into their own dark and lonely world. The hopelessness that I felt for them did not compare to the tidal wave of utter devastation that washed over me when I showed them Kristin's graduation picture. One of the girls recognized Kristin and turned around and pointed saying, "She works that corner over there." I felt like my life had just come to an end.

After a period of feeling paralyzed I gathered myself and put my detective skills to work to find and save our daughter.

Chapter 6 Nobody Puts Baby in a Corner

Vancouver, B.C. 2000

We quickly came to the conclusion that Kristin was using home as a soft landing to temporarily escape from her drug-crazed world. She would be home, compliant, helpful, and repentant for about a week and then disappear again. My well-meaning AA friends beat the drums of "she'll get help when she wants to get help." Tough love advocates offered the back door policy to her so that she would be forced to get assistance. And there were the gracious Christian folks who offered sympathy, care and patience along with listening ears. I often felt like a magician sticking my hand deeply in a hat hoping to pull out the appropriate strategy. Our wide swings of plans and manners dealing with Kristin must have been confusing to her. I kept thinking that no one gets up in the morning and decides to become a heroin addict, an alcoholic or one who puts up with mental, emotional and sexual abuse. I asked the questions, I read the books, and I continued to come up with few answers. In the darkest hours of my not knowing what to do or where to turn, I only knew that God was still with me. I told Him my thoughts, my fears and my questions. I didn't receive any real answers, but I received His presence and assurance that He was silently at work. Kristin's life was a revolving door between drug abuse, rehabilitation centers and home. The process was exhausting to all of us, especially Kristin.

In 2000, Jerry was called to a church in Southern California. Our entire family saw this as an opportunity to begin a fresh chapter in our life and to give Kristin the chance to make some significant adjustments. Kristin seemed to be excited about the move and though there were a few rough times, months went by with fewer anxious moments. Jerry needed to report for his new position so he and Jon moved to California ahead of the rest of the family. The plan was for me to come to California with both girls as soon as our house sold. Jana was still in school, I was teaching and Kristin was helping me around the house. We often talked about fresh starts, a new job and the overall opportunity to make a life change. There was definitely excitement in the air. All three of us girls were looking forward to the plane ride to California and a change in our life.

I had finished the dishes one particular evening and after helping Jana with her homework, I went to bed fully expecting Kristin to come in from seeing her girlfriend. I fell asleep and was wakened by the telephone ringing next to my ear. Kristin was on the other end of the phone asking for a ride home from Vancouver. It was two a.m. and Jana was sleeping. I heard the anxious tone in Kristin's voice and asked her where she was and why she hadn't come home sooner. She replied saying that the buses stopped running and she was at an AA meeting downtown Vancouver on Oak Street. I told her to wait and I would soon be there to pick her up. I called a friend to come over and be there in case Jana woke up. After my friend arrived, I left for downtown. I picked up Kristin and could tell that she was high. The ride home was filled with tense conversation and I finally told Kristin that she was never to go to Vancouver again without me. She wasn't to go with a friend, with a relative, with a policeman. In fact, I even said if Jesus asks you to go with Him to Vancouver, I want you to come and get me first! I reminded her that we were moving in two weeks and that this was her chance to begin life over with a new focus. She nodded her head in agreement. As we turned the corner onto our suburban street, she looked at me and said, "Mom, I won't go to Vancouver unless I take a friend and we go to a meeting." I could hardly believe my ears. I stomped on the brake nearly sending her flying into the front window. "Look at me, Kristin…let me make it perfectly clear. You are never to go to Vancouver again for any reason and if you do go, it will tell me that you really don't want to move with us to California. Is that clear?" Kristin gave me a look of compliance yet with vague and murky understanding. The next morning, I went to work and when I came home from school, there was a note on the kitchen table that said the following:

Mom,
I went to Vancouver. I'll be back later.
Love,
Kristin

I was shocked and in disbelief as I stared at the note. What was she thinking? How could she write this and think everything would be alright? I was certain that she got the message just the night before that she was NOT to go to Vancouver for any reason. I went to bed that night but there was no phone call and no Kristin. By 7 in the morning, I checked Kristin's room and she was sleeping. I woke her up and asked to speak with her downstairs. The following conversation had lasting implications that I think about to this very day. I called Jerry and we agreed on the plan that I laid out to Kristin. I told her that May 18 was the day that Jana and I were moving to California to join Dad and Jon. We were taking a plane trip that day. It was the morning of May 8, 2000 and I told her that she had a choice to make. She could pack some things in a suitcase and take the bus down to California that day and begin rehabilitation there or pack some things and return to Vancouver. If she chose the second option she was not moving to California with us.

As I laid out the plan, I believed tough love was justifiably spilling out deliberately and forcefully. I felt betrayed, angered and unwilling to allow her to take part in the same moving arrangements as Jana and me. I knew she needed help desperately and I did not know what to do. Bewildered by the circumstance, I honestly did not know what her choice was going to be. She turned around and went upstairs and I could hear her busily putting things in place to make her move. What would her destination be? Her life was coming down to one huge decision and I believed that I was helping her to make the right choice. After about an hour, I went upstairs and peered into her room. I watched for a minute or so as she put some clothes in her bag. I asked her where she was going. She seriously looked at me and answered, "I'm going to Vancouver." My mouth went dry. I could barely speak. My world was in slow motion. Like actors rehearsing lines, I said, "You are choosing to move away from your family. Kristin, repeat after me, 'I'd rather live with Sam than my family.'" She looked squarely into my face and calmly said, "I'd rather live with Sam than my family." That was it. I had tried to back her into a corner to make a right decision and then I watched silently and helplessly as she walked out the door. Some unknown guy pulled up in front in a beat up truck and the door swung open and Kristin hopped in and that truck drove away with my firstborn. I had no tears left.

Jana and I boarded a plane and moved to the L.A. area. Three months later in Vancouver, Kristin turned twenty-five. I have no memories of that birthday. Where she was or how she spent her birthday was unknown. Life in California was busy and much simpler without the drug drama in our home. Each day I woke up believing that we would receive a phone call from Kristin telling us how she had decided to get help and to move forward with her life. But each day passed in deafening silence. We learned that Kristin continued to keep in touch with several of our friends in our small Vancouver suburb. They would call and we would listen to accounts of how she showed up at their door, cold, asking for food or money. Once one of her cousins thought for sure she had seen Kristin on a news show when a story was featured about the homeless in East Vancouver. We were trying our best to live with the fact that one of our children was destroying herself. We felt completely helpless to do anything to stop her. Personally, I felt like I was among the walking dead. It was difficult to concentrate and when I was alone in my thoughts, I was desperate. Where was she? Was she warm enough? Did she have food? What in the world was going on?

That October, I was asked to come to Vancouver Island to speak at a women's conference. I shared my own heavy heart and honestly asked for prayer and support. Many other women commiserated with me regarding children with drug problems. I investigated and found out where Kristin's last address was in the city. I called and told the front desk clerk of the old dismal downtown hotel that I was Kristin's mother and would like to speak to her. I got a curt reply that no such person lived there. I waited about an hour and called back and said that I needed to come by and bring Kristin some money that I owed her. The same voice perked up this time and said, "She usually is here around 2." So...I went down to the hotel and opened up the creaky front door and stuck my head into the office. I said, "I'm a friend of Kristin's...is she still in the same room or did she move?" The scruffy looking man said, "Same room... upstairs to the right. Number 214." My heart was pounding as I climbed the broken stairs and turned the corner. I hadn't seen my daughter since May 8. I saw the number over the door jam and I knocked a brisk pattern on the dingy painted door. I heard rumbling and rustling and feet hitting the floor. I heard the lock as it jiggled and the door opened. Sam stood in front of me eye to eye and he stared and said, "Oh my God." I said, "No, it isn't God...it's me. I want to see Kristin." Kristin heard my voice and came running out and nearly knocked me over. She hugged and kissed me over and over again. We both cried with sheer joy. She told me how good I smelled and she kept kissing me on the cheek and the hands. The three of us went back into the room and I sat on the end of the bed while Sam got into the bed wearing the maroon bathrobe that we had bought for Kristin the previous Christmas when she was in rehab. The moment felt surreal. I could hardly believe where I was or that the three of us were together in this dumpy hotel room. She asked about Jon and Jana. She wanted to know about Dad and told me how much she missed all of us. I looked around at the dirty room and saw a can of soup that had been opened sitting on a hot plate. As I spoke and tried my best to explain what I thought was going on, Kristin and Sam just stared at me with the look of confusion and shame. We talked for awhile and made a date to meet again the next morning. I told her that I had a plane ticket for her to go home with me. She looked excited and told me she would pack and be ready for me the next morning. I was elated and yet cautious in my feelings. I so wanted her to be able to get out of this hole.

The next morning, I excitedly packed and drove to the city and waited outside for Kristin to come out. She came out and popped into the car and gave me a hug. We talked and then the conversation went sideways. She said that she needed to pack more of her clothes, to say good bye to her friends, and take care of a couple of things before she came to California. It sounded and looked like a bad B movie. She jumped out of the car in the rain and waved good-bye and said that she would come in a couple of weeks. When she ran down the alley and behind the building I knew she wouldn't be coming to California any time soon. Her behavior had always produced a jumbled concoction of sadness and anger in me. This time was no different for me. I started the car and drove to the airport. The road looked blurry though my tears.

Months went by without a word from Kristin. By the end of March we could not stand the pain one more day. There were a few connections made between us and yet a giant wall seemed to separate us. We encouraged her to move closer to us and receive the help she needed. But she could not bring herself to make the trip. Jerry had begun a new job and needed to pay attention to his responsibilities. But with a growing sense of anguish, Jerry asked for time off and flew to Vancouver to find Kristin again. The dingy hotel where I had seen her just months before had burned down. She relocated to another cockroach infested flat. Jerry found her and took her away to Whistler where they stayed in a beautiful cabin for the week. He said that they talked, ate great meals, walked and basically reconnected as a Daddy and daughter once again. Jerry went with the sole purpose of serving Kristin. He wanted her to feel the love that he had for her. He personally gave her manicures and pedicures after washing her feet and hands. Living in the street culture of Vancouver had its impact on her appearance as well as her social mores and style. He lovingly cared for her dirty, broken body hoping that his love would penetrate her hurting heart. He washed and tinted and cut her hair for her and gave her facials. A local beauty salon would have done a more professional job but her own Dad's loving hands were what her broken spirit needed. Jerry noticed that Kristin had a slight inability to connect, track and to feel. By the end of the week, he thought she was a little more like herself. She was smiling more, asking questions and showing affection for him like days gone by. During the end of their time together, they talked about Kristin joining him on his trip home. Jerry told her how much we all missed her, how that we all loved her and how much we all longed to see her get the right kind of help that she needed. He committed our family to her to stand with her and by her to love and resource her in the best way possible. It was a wonderful week.

Jerry called me in an emotional state on his way to the airport as he described to me yet another aborted mission to get Kristin out of the drug-infested city. Many attempts to contact her followed that visit but each attempt was met with no success in finding Kristin. It was like she had disappeared. No phone calls. No letters. No connection at all. Besides the frightening thoughts of where she might be, I hated the new feeling of numbness and distance that I was beginning to feel. The time and space between us and our daughter sadly was beginning to feel normal. Could this be what death feels like?

Chapter 7 The Rescue

California 2001

On a Monday evening six weeks after Jerry's trip to Vancouver to serve Kristin I got a call from our son, Jon. As he matured into a young man, Jon became an admired peer for both Jerry and me. He was wise beyond his years and had an understanding of people and circumstances that was amazing. He was a strong 23 year old young man with love for his sister and a passion to help her. Jon had his own normal growing up issues and wasn't a stranger to experimenting with drugs or alcohol, but never to the extent of Kristin's involvement. Jon had moved to Santa Barbara and was living on his own learning the electrical trade. Living independently made Jon a mature and caring individual.

I answered the call and heard a message from Jon that turned out to be a catalyst to change our lives and Kristin's life too. Jon spoke confidently and forcefully that he believed God was telling him to go and bring Kristin home from Vancouver. I was intrigued but my broken heart had been hardened over the years by many vain attempts to offer her help. I listened and learned that he wanted to fly that Thursday to Vancouver. His plan was to bring her home from whenever he found her. He booked off the time at work and asked us for assistance to make the trip. We hurriedly made arrangements acquiring a plane ticket, hotel, car and Kristin's passport. While he was gone we agreed to become the babysitters for his dog, Chica. He scoured the family picture album and chose Kristin's high school graduation picture to take with him. That same picture had been used many times before to locate her. It was time to bring it out once again. He boarded the plane with the well worn picture in his back pocket and confidence that he would bring Kristin home with him.

Jon landed in Vancouver at 7 p.m. that Thursday evening in June. Miraculously, we got a phone call from him at 8:30 p.m. telling us that he was holding Kristin in his arms. No one could have convinced me that God didn't exist at that moment. No one.

Jon had taken the picture with him to East Vancouver and began showing it to various 7-11 stores, newspaper stands, Starbucks, doughnut shops, and people standing around the street corners. He started out getting blank stares and then one comment came after his request of, "Do you know this girl?" "I don't know her, but the guy two blocks that way knows her, I think." The trail started to quicken. "I don't know her, but the guy over there does." "I saw her once, but I don't know her." Finally, someone led Jon to a rescue mission in downtown Vancouver. He went in and convinced the receptionist that he was Kristin's brother and he had come from California to visit her. After some anxious moments, the staff member at the mission detox center came out leading Kristin. She was wearing a hospital gown looking skinny, sick, confused, and scared. When Jon took her in his arms he felt confirmation about his mission. Kristin had trouble feeling anything. She later told me that she wasn't certain who it was that was holding her, but the familiar family smell told her it was either Dad or Jon. Kristin had been dropped on the door step of the mission only a few days before Jon's arrival. She was found lying on park bench in downtown Vancouver shivering cold, hungry and completely alone. The next several days were filled with Jon carefully putting together plans to take Kristin with him to California. The risky mission required the proper identification and official documents to declare that Jon was someone to be trusted to take Kristin out of Canada. Medical doctors needed to sign off on her medical condition in order to release her. She also needed some medication to enable her to cope with the detoxification process. Each of these action points had time frames that needed to be observed and Jon was kept busy each day carrying out the plans for his sister.

Monday became the planned travel day for Kristin and Jon. He made a trip to a department store and bought underwear, bra, pants, blouse, shoes and of course a purse for Kristin. He bought her some make up, shampoo and a brush for her to put in her purse and then took all of the items to the detox center to give to Kristin. With all of the proper papers in hand, Jon asked for her release from the center. He signed the papers while Kristin put on her new clothes and readied herself to leave. They released Kristin at 6:00 p.m. and the two walked out of the center into the rainy Vancouver weather and into the borrowed car. Jon drove as Kristin sat in the passenger's seat. She became restless and finally adamant about getting out of the car. "I can't go with you. I have to go downtown. Let me out." she whined. Jon strategically kept driving and talking to her very calmly, but with determination. He drove for hours not always even knowing where he was. He kept giving Kristin hope by buying her fast food or snacks and finally finding a source to buy some marijuana to calm her down. He bought gas and drove some more. He drove all night until seven that next morning. After being angry and agitated for most of the night, Kristin finally fell asleep against the car window and Jon drove carefully back to the hotel.

As she slept, Jon carried her into the hotel room. He carefully laid her down on the bed and he pulled the cabinet in front of the door to barricade Kristin and himself in the room. He stayed awake as long as he could and finally fell asleep in a chair beside the bed. By noon, Jon was up and promising Kristin a fresh cup of coffee and a cinnamon bun to help her start the day. He gingerly took each step of the trip to the airport making no fast or harsh turns. That night Jon won the trust of his sister and together they boarded the flight to LAX at 3:00 the next afternoon. Once on the plane, Jon tried to relax his body but his mind was racing with what could be done for his edgy sister who slept next to him.

When Kristin and Jon came walking off of the airplane at LAX that evening, Kristin shuffled awkwardly ahead of her brother with bandages covering her hands and parts of her face. Her thin, tired body tipped the scales at barely 100 pounds. Her 5′5″ athletic body had disappeared into an emaciated, cocaine skeleton draped with sallow, translucent skin. Her once beautifully thick, brunette head of hair now lay lifeless and twisted around her sad face. My husband, Jerry and I anxiously waited for our oldest daughter and son to come home to us. We were nervous, but so excited to have our dear Kristin home with us to complete and restore our family. Jon walked behind her with a look of uneasiness written on his face shaking his head back and forth. To us Kristin looked like a frightened, vulnerable little animal as she drew back with a look of bewilderment and desperation. In that moment I couldn't help but feel sorry for myself. My own daughter didn't seem to know who I was.

After embracing our two oldest children with feelings of profound gratitude and pain, we watched Jon drive his old battered red truck out of the airport parking lot carrying Kristin…the precious cargo we had all sought to recover. The California sun set on that strange looking entourage. As they disappeared from sight, our hearts were lifted when we saw Jon's dog Chica's ears flapping happily in the wind. Jon's quiet neighborhood in Santa Barbara seemed to be the perfect setting for Kristin to rest and renew her spirit. That summer became a team effort to take care of Kristin. Jerry spent the week with Kristin in Santa Barbara as Jon went to work. I remained home with Jana. We soon discovered that Kristin had suffered significant emotional deterioration since the last time Jerry saw her in Vancouver just a few weeks prior. She could not mentally track or focus on a subject. She wandered in bizarre tangents in her thinking and verbiage. She used words and confused them with one another which made it extremely difficult to follow. She had little modesty and would often need to be reminded to wear clothing. Her social skills were nearly nonexistent and she required a constant chaperone so as not to be misunderstood in a public situation. She could not be trusted to be alone or even left to take a walk by herself for fear of getting lost. We watched her as she mumbled to herself and made gestures as though she were speaking with someone. She could not carry on a clear conversation and she was often stuck on imagining spiritual cataclysmic events. She spoke to each of us in the family in an authoritative way reminding us that she was Jesus and that she wanted to save each of us from the impending doom. Her pieces of advice made no sense and had no connection to reality. She smoked incessantly and didn't have the awareness of where to deposit her ashes. She ate her food hungrily and fast like a starving animal and she was obsessive in asking for what she needed. Whether it was food, clothing, shampoo, coffee, cigarettes or soda pop, she needed it and she needed it now.

One week when Jerry was with Kristin, he decided it was time to take her to the county offices in Santa Barbara and have her evaluated for assistance both medically and financially. He took her to the County of Santa Barbara Department of Health Care Services on Camino Del Remedio. They walked in and were able to get an appointment with a staff member. Departments of Mental Health and Drug Abuse are dually established under one organizational umbrella in California. This was a fact that we did not know at the time. In Jerry's mind he was taking Kristin into the building to get a medical evaluation and help for a loved one coming off of heavy street drugs. Jerry and Kristin were led into a room so that a staff member could speak with Kristin and get the appropriate information. Jerry explained to his best ability the events that brought Kristin down to California. He was interested in finding out what kind of assistance she was eligible for because she was not able to work. Were there programs designed to assist her in recovery and get back into society? The young male staff member began to interview Kristin and asked some leading questions as to her thinking ability. "What do you like to do in your spare time? Where would you go to spend time?" Kristin mentioned the beach and the water. Jon had taken her to the beach many times over the summer. Her mind started to wander and she spoke about walking into the water. The evaluator asked about the wounds on her hands and face and Kristin said that she got burned from her cigarette. It was at that point that the conversation took a turn. The evaluator said, "Kristin, I think you need to go into the hospital for a little while and get feeling better, don't you?" The evaluator looked cautiously at Jerry. Kristin said, "Oh, I don't know about that." Then, she turned to Jerry and said, "I want to call Jon." So, Jerry took out his cell phone and dialed Jon at work. Jon wisely said, "Well Kristin, what do you think? Do you think you could use the rest and help in a hospital for a little while?" Kristin said, "Maybe that would be good, Jon." Then she put the phone down and said, "Yeah, I think I will go into the hospital for awhile, Dad. But first, I want to go home to Jon's and get my shampoo." Jerry thought this was a great idea and the two of them stood up and started to leave when around the corner came several large uniformed policemen who grabbed Kristin and jerked her away from Jerry. Kristin began to scream, "Daddy, Daddy….no, no, no. Help me Daddy." Jerry stood there in shock and disbelief that his daughter was being torn from his arms and pulled into a waiting police car out front. The evaluator calmly told Jerry that because of the interview, he determined that she was in danger of hurting others or herself with the obvious proof of the self inflicted wounds on her body. He called the process a 51-50 which is taking someone against their will because of the threat of hurting themselves or others. Jerry stood with his mouth wide open and his heart broken in two knowing that all of the weeks of care and love shown to Kristin to build trust had been broken down in the space of about five minutes. He watched as the car pulled away with lights flashing and Kristin screaming in the back seat like a frightened slave. Jerry came for help and the public system took his daughter from him. Kristin's street memories of policemen were being relived at that moment of panic.

Jerry demanded answers and got very few. He called me and I dropped everything and drove to Santa Barbara. The next morning, Jerry, Jon and I went to the mental health hospital where Kristin was confined and talked to the psychiatrist in charge. We got a fast tracked education on who is legally in charge of someone who is over the age of 18 in California. Kristin being 25 was no longer under her parents' legal custody. Though we explained the situation for well over an hour, it appeared that Kristin was going to have to stay and have more evaluations before being released. We suspected that her drug use had altered her brain and her thinking processes. However pulling her away from her parents' arms was not helping her trust nor was it providing her with the hope of healing. The doctor diagnosed Kristin's condition as a combination of drug abuse and mental illness. As he tried to explain it to us we could only think about our daughter and her lack of trust in us. I finally made the statement that I would just stay at the hospital until Kristin could come out. I would either sleep in the hallway or they could give me a bed next to Kristin's in the ward. The doctor looked stunned and asked if I was serious. I said that I had never been more serious in my life. Jon, Jerry and I stood shoulder to shoulder facing the doctor pleading for her release. I'm not sure if it was the promise of getting me as a "guest" at his hospital or not but the doctor ordered Kristin's papers and prepared for her release to us. We signed the papers with a promise that we would get her the appropriate mental health help along with drug rehabilitation.

We walked into the hospital ward to reclaim Kristin who was standing by her hospital bed. A child's coloring book was open to a scribbled page on the hospital bed tray. She turned around and was quietly responsive to us. I'm sure she had been heavily medicated. She dressed with very little to say and the four of us left the hospital with the first of many disconcerting memories of getting help from the state and county mental health departments in our hearts. We were all confused.

Chapter 8 Nine Eleven

California September 11, 2001

We searched and investigated various drug rehabilitation facilities in the area for Kristin. We were determined to find just the right place that would truly help Kristin. We brought her from her brother's apartment in Santa Barbara to live with us in Huntington Beach. As the days passed, she allowed her trust to grow once again. I asked her to write down her thoughts during this time to remind herself of what she would like to talk about. She seemed happy to do that. The first thing that she wrote on a piece of tablet paper was completely unreadable. There were letters and symbols, but very few words.

July 10, 2001

In & sleep, an outhous dims, it crofto cluel-
dawell toz tado kipl can us folo allow
lace cane plait don't cauke/e osespia

Tight, close imparts wormed miney Closures.
at last!! = marker whims wose I said.
To slot a bon makes a wan. Sought
alreigh to watch is for 'OH God revels gerumy
when calming comes.

In nin a poc sd, well walk or shop
Col with yeh (gitty) residents

I couldn't believe my eyes. She had lost her ability to either read or write. Her speech was jumbled, illogical and disjointed. Her attention span was very short. She was more interested in talking to those who were only present in her mind than those of us who surrounded her with love. Our daughter was deeply disturbed and it was heartbreaking for us to observe her.

By this time, Kristin had already lived in at least 10 different drug rehabilitation facilities. To even bring up the subject of yet another program was answered with a defiant "No." We carefully approached the issue of getting on to the next part of her life and she seemed interested. Kristin was always a hard worker and could outwork most men. She had done manual labor in several of the drug facilities in Canada. She was used to working so she wanted a job. We took her to a highly acclaimed drug rehabilitation center in San Clemente. Jerry, Jana and I went to visitor's day and also took some classes for family members of a drug addict. She lasted almost a month and we got the call. We were told that Kristin was a lovely girl and that she wanted to improve; however she just could not seem to do the required paperwork or logically work the 12-step program. It was no mystery to us that she could not do the paper work. At this point in her rehabilitation she was unable to read or write. She needed help. If she did not fit into a top -ranked rehabilitation center, where did she fit? As we drove once again to pick Kristin up from a rehabilitation facility, we felt frustrated and at a loss to know what to do next. On the way home we tried to encourage her by telling her how proud we were of her and reassuring her that she had not done anything to break the rules. We truly hoped that she was making progress and was beginning to improve. We just needed to find the appropriate place for her.

Communicating with Kristin became one of our biggest challenges. We sincerely wanted her to understand that we loved her, that we wanted to help her and that we were with her for the long road to find her way back. Kristin had seen a psychiatrist while she was at the Drug Rehabilitation center and we decided to make an appointment with that doctor to get his diagnosis of her. We wondered if he would have some clues to Kristin's recovery. The doctor's office set the appointment time for September 11, 2001 at 8:00. We left early that morning and stopped at a local convenience store to buy a newspaper so that Jana could get an article for Junior High. As we walked in to the store, the friendly Iranian clerk began loudly and nervously talking to me telling me to turn on the radio. There was a terrible event happening in New York City. We got back into the car and tuned on the radio and learned of America's horrific national tragedy. The twin towers in New York City had been hit by two commercial airplanes and were twin towering infernos.

Our country was in total confusion and mourning as we dropped Jana at her school. We stayed glued to the radio as we continued on to San Clemente to the psychiatrist's office. When we arrived at the doctor's office, the same radio station was broadcasting the latest details. We waited and talked about the horror while Kristin smoked a cigarette outside completely oblivious to the events of the morning. The doctor spent some time talking with Kristin and then asked us to come into his office for a private consultation. Kristin was relieved to be able to go outside and smoke once again. The doctor gave us his professional diagnosis: Kristin had a definite mental illness. The doctor called the illness Schizophrenia and told us that the disease was one that was congenital, meaning that it was present at birth. He said that the disease did not show up until later adolescence and that most people did not experience any symptoms until their late teens or early twenties. He continued with the devastating prognosis that this was a long term illness and could not be cured. The best we could hope for would be treatment with certain medications, and he cautioned us that it was a long road to learn the ideal balance of prescriptions. Then he looked at us over the top of his glasses and said, "You are loving parents. This is something that comes from no fault of yours or your daughter. Drugs did not do this to her. She probably used drugs when the disease showed up to self-medicate. Do not take a second mortgage out on your home thinking you can fix this with expensive treatments. This is definitely a long-term illness and you will need to help her for the rest of her life." I felt like those words were cutting through me like a knife. The room was beginning to spin. I couldn't even respond. As the world watched the fiery demolition in New York City, we felt like our lives were simultaneously being dismantled along with the towers. Our daughter was mentally ill. The news made us feel sick.

After hearing the doctor's diagnosis, we immediately made plans to see other doctors for a second opinion on Kristin's status. Every doctor who saw her and interviewed her gave the same diagnosis. Schizophrenia. I had heard that word before and thought that it had something to do with a split personality…whatever that meant. I looked it up on the web and read books and articles to help me understand the daughter that I had given birth to 25 years prior. I watched the Academy Award winning movie, "A Beautiful Mind" and cried though most of it as I related Kristin to the feelings of the main character. There was nothing beautiful about Schizophrenia.

Chapter 9 The Rabbit's Hole

Kristin lived in the spare bedroom upstairs next to Jana's room. We gave her the prescribed medications and looked for improvement. She slept a lot, smoked a lot, and wasn't interested in television or much of anything for that matter. She talked about drugs and what she would do if someone offered her some. We believed that she was a drug addict with a mental illness. Kristin could not work so we applied for Social Security Insurance which is a government-funded stipend for those who are unable to work. Kristin and I went to the Social Security office where Kristin was once again interviewed. When asked questions, she would often look at me with tired eyes like she was saying, "Why does everyone ask me the same things over and over?" Kristin was classified as mentally disabled and was given the standard monthly allowance to help with her expenses.

With a deep sense of loss blanketing us, we tried to continue on with life as best as we could. Jon came to visit often to reassure Kristin of his love and devotion. Jana in early adolescence at thirteen began to be the big sister to her 25 year old sibling. This was not the family dynamic Jana had signed up for in our household. Like a wheel out of balance our family went wobbling down life's road.

One Sunday night, Jerry and I were away at a church meeting when I called home and talked to Jana. I asked her if she wanted us to pick her up some fast food on our way home. She said, "Yes, that would be great." I asked if Kristin would want some. Jana agreed that Kristin was also hungry and that she had been in her bedroom all evening. We bought the burgers and headed for home. It was a cold and rainy winter night and as we turned into the driveway, we saw a police car parked in front of our house with the lights flashing. The garage door was open. Jana was standing at the back door and Kristin was sitting on the back step. The policeman was standing over Kristin talking to her. As our car lights lit up the garage, Jana looked at us with disgust and turned around and slammed the back door to the house leaving Kristin and the policeman in full view. The policeman told us that Kristin had gone out without telling Jana and began jogging on Pacific Coast Highway. She had fallen down narrowly missing some speeding cars. A concerned motorist called the police and they picked her up. The responding officer asked Kristin her name and she told them. He asked her what her address was and she said that she did not know. She also did not know the phone number. The policeman finally found the house by locating our name and brought her home. When they arrived at the house, the police asked Jana if Kristin was on drugs because of her odd behavior. Before she could answer we arrived and Jana left the scene. By the time we explained the situation and how sorry we were that we allowed such a thing to happen and promised that it would not happen again, the police left and the burgers were more than cold. Jana was in tears telling us how the whole incident scared her to death. Jana protested that she could not be responsible for a twenty-five year old woman who could not think for herself. Jana was right. Meanwhile, Kristin thought there was too much made out of the event. She considered it to be a minor incident of jogging, getting a bit lost and falling down. She ate her hamburger and went to bed. We knew that we needed to do something else for Kristin. We just did not know what to do. Once again, Kristin's behavior was making life difficult for everyone in our family.

In an effort to seek help we made many trips to look for drug rehabilitation facilities and spent many sleepless nights. Our family became a corps of watchmen as we would take turns making sure Kristin was still in the house. Through some incredible generosity of friends, we moved Kristin into a pricey special treatment facility in Costa Mesa for youth and adults. Many of the clients were dual diagnosis with a history of drug addiction and mental illness. That treatment facility lasted about two months. Soon Kristin was home again wondering where she belonged. The staff psychologist at the facility gave us a long printed report on Kristin that detailed her aberrant behavior but did not provide any direction or help for the future. She would not obey rules, she heard voices, she would not attend meetings regularly, and she would not do the paper work. In the psychologist's opinion, she was not able to complete the program. I wondered what Kristin was feeling as she heard another harsh critique. We felt the sting of failure at every turn. Where was the promise of progress or the road to improvement that the doctor had sold? Kristin was fully medicated at the levels psychiatry prescribed for mental illness, yet she was not making the progress.

Within a few weeks of Kristin's release we learned of a house in San Diego for female drug addicts who also had some mental issues. We drove there and Kristin was interviewed once again. She was admitted so we packed her things and left her at the little Victorian house feeling hopeful that this was the place. Alice, the director, was a precious woman who loved her girls and wanted them to improve and get back into society. The mental diagnosis of Schizophrenia did not seem to scare her and we were thrilled. Kristin was there for only a couple of days when she walked off the property and caught a bus for home. The only problem with that was she took a city bus and got as far as the outskirts of San Diego. She called our home. She wanted to come home and she did not want to be taken to another facility. She did not want any help. She just wanted to be home. We thought that her inability to finish a program was just Kristin being her stubborn self again. How could she manage to take a bus and make a phone call but could not seem to follow through on what she needed to do? It was all so bewildering. We told her to go back to Alice's place. She indeed needed a place with a staff of people who knew how to deal with her and her mental illness. When she hung up, I was desperate and cried out to God, "Help her. No one else seems to be able to do anything. Please. Help her."

Kristin got on a bus and went to Scripps Mercy Hospital in San Diego. She admitted herself there and said that she needed help. She was put into the psychiatric ward of the hospital and the doctor there took an interest in Kristin and allowed her to stay for three months which is about four times longer than usual for mentally ill patients. There is a God.

At Scripps, Kristin had more medications prescribed, cognitive therapy administered and had an MRI taken of her brain. The doctor told me that he definitely saw something different in Kristin and he wanted to help. We believed for the first time that we were getting some real help for Kristin. At first, she was always in bed when we came to visit. She did not say much. She just breathed. Her eyes were dull and her hands were quivering and shaky. She sometimes stumbled when she walked. The doctor assured us that she was being stabilized on her medication but that there were some side effects from them. It was described as a very fragile process to get the psychotropic drugs monitored in Kristin. After the three months the doctor advised us to put Kristin in a long-term dual diagnosis facility where they are trained to treat former addicts who also suffer with a mental condition.

In October of 2002, Kristin was admitted to Alpine Dual Diagnosis Center east of San Diego. While she was there our family visited at least once a month taking her out for lunch, coffee, or shopping. Patients were offered three different levels of care and when one graduated from the third level, they were released. The program worked toward the goal of reentering society. Inside the facility it was a strange beehive of activity. There was a cage like patio for smoke breaks. Patients shared bedrooms and bathrooms. Women and men were on the same floor living in bedrooms right next to each other. Though the doors were locked, there seemed to be great accountability and caring staff at the facility. Each week a psychiatrist, a nutritionist and an exercise program director worked with Kristin. They expected Kristin to work hard on her improvement.

We discovered that progress is often three steps forward and two steps backwards. After a few weeks Kristin moved up a level. Then we got a call one day telling us that Kristin was put back in her level of care. She had a confrontation with another patient on the smoking patio. A young man called another female patient "Fatty" which made Kristin defensive for the girl. Kristin told the man he would be sorry if he ever said that again. When he made the same derogatory remark, Kristin walked over and slugged him so solidly on the chin that he dropped to the patio. Kristin used her strength to defend a girl against an epithet that brought back unhappy memories in her childhood. When the incident was reported to me I was not too disappointed in what she had done. It told me that she was thinking and starting to feel. Good for her.

Kristin stayed for two years at the Dual Diagnosis Center in Alpine, California. During that time she had three conservators who are representatives appointed by the court to make decisions for Kristin. I volunteered to be the conservator but to my surprise Kristin told the judge that she didn't want me as her conservator. Ironically, Kristin ultimately made the decision that said she could not make a decision as to how she would make decisions. Even more ironic, the court let the decision stand. I was beginning to wonder, "Who was the one needing mental assistance? Who's crazy now?" The day after the court appointed a conservator, Kristin asked me if I was the one who would be her conservator. I reminded her of what she decided in court. She did not understand the legal process and, frankly, neither did I. For the next two years Kristin had three different conservators who had little time to give. We saw few positive results of having an overworked and stressed-out public conservator manage Kristin's affairs.

Jerry and I continued to visit Kristin and take her out for the day. Little by little we could see her "stabilize" on the medications. One day after visiting Kristin the door locked behind me and I was walking to the car asking myself if we were witnessing the institutionalization of Kristin Rueb. She paced the halls incessantly listening to her walkman. She shuffled along the hallways not talking to anyone, but looking lost and vacant. She was becoming more and more compliant, but she hardly resembled herself. Her entire body shook and her appearance took a real turn toward the worse. She began to rapidly gain weight yet she was walking constantly and eating nutritious meals. We witnessed our daughter becoming more mentally ill with each passing day. She got clothes out of the giveaway box and dressed in outfits that were most unusual, to put it mildly. One day I arrived to take her out for lunch. Her beautiful hair was cut in a style that resembled a Mohawk Indian. She had on very short and tight pink shorts with a tight red top. Fingernail polish was painted on her lips and dark black eye makeup was smeared all over and under her eyes. Oddly, she seemed to be happy with the look. There were times that I asked her to make an improvement to her style. Other times, it just didn't seem important.

The facility maintained a two year limit for anyone in residence there. When Kristin was admitted we got the impression that it was a long-term facility. We assumed that patients were released when they were able to renter society. We were in for a rude awakening. The fact was that the Social Security Insurance benefit was only good for a two-year period at that facility. After two years patients were required to leave and make room for another resident. It was a wake-up call on how little assistance there is for a mentally challenged adult. Even after two years, Kristin was not ready to live on her own. She was not able to take her own medication without monitoring, she could not work or look after herself, yet the facility deemed her "cured" and released her. The court ruled that she no longer needed a conservator. We were back at square one. Kristin came home for a few weeks and we revived our search for the next step in her recovery.

As word got out to family, friends, and acquaintances that Kristin was home but not cured we began to hear from people who had connections with those facing similar challenges. When new suggestions were proposed we were skeptical but still desperate to find an answer. There were cowboy ranches in Wyoming for juvenile delinquents, hiking expeditions for troubled teens and programs where mentally disabled children worked filling jars with buttons to gain spending money. Where was the place that truly fit Kristin? She was 28 years old, but responded like an early teenager. She was a young woman with dreams, hopes and memories but not at home in her own body and brain. She was trying to improve without treatment so we were not about to give up. I pulled out the thank you note that she printed and sent to me while she was living in San Diego. I could

Aug 10, 2004

Oh man I miss being with all you. I had such a good time. I'll see you first Mom. I'm doing well and waiting for Sept 9 for when I leave.

Love,

Kristin

see real change from the garbled message that she wrote that first summer after coming to California. Slowly she was making progress, yet the opportunities around her were staying the same.

A staff member at the Social Security office who

visited yearly to check on Kristin's status gave me stale information on web sites, places and organizations that were very little or no help at all. After visiting several private drug treatment centers it became very apparent to us that Kristin was no longer wanting to do drugs but needed something very different, yet very specific. Wanting Kristin to be nearer to us, we looked and found no care facilities here in Huntington Beach. We were given a list of room and board facilities by the department of mental health and finally moved Kristin into a house in Anaheim. The facility consisted of two suburban houses across the street from one another with about six clients total living in the two houses. The clients ate on the patio outside of one of the houses and though it was clean and seemed to be safe and appropriate, my heart was aching when I left that evening knowing that Kristin was eating outside in the middle of winter with a group of troubled adults while I was driving home to our warm and comfortable home. I was grateful that Anaheim, California has a warm climate; however, the arrangement, though it was the best we visited, was not what I had in mind for her. To her credit Kristin learned to be a survivor and did not usually balk at what we offered to her. She wanted to be at home but she seemed to accept the fact that she needed supervision which was something we were not able to give her consistently. In her new surroundings she had a room to herself and so she was thrilled. The staff person at the house was very friendly to her and I believed that this might be the place that Kristin could gain independence and even find a part-time job. Kristin was there for four months but one weekend while Kristin was visiting Jon, she came home to find her belongings in boxes in the garage. The facility owner wanted Kristin's room for another client so she moved her belongings. The landlord had another house with a room for Kristin and so we helped her move once more. She was in the new house for a very short time and another client offered Kristin cough syrup and beer and the two of them were asked to leave the house. We looked and found another house not far away and moved her there. Kristin was asked to leave because she did not follow house rules which consisted of keeping the back door shut, smoking only outside and properly closing the cereal boxes. Her case worker at the Anaheim Mental Health Center found another room and board facility for her living arrangements. At that level of care, a room and food to eat is provided but the client must be responsible to take their own medications. Some clients even had part-time jobs. This new setting gave me hope that at some point Kristin would find a job. But Kristin was unable to administer her own medications so an even higher level of care was proposed. The county case worker found a board and care facility where the staff managed each client's medications. Kristin lasted for only two months in the board and care facility because she did not follow the rules. Once again she was asked to leave.

At least once a month I took Kristin to her mental health appointment at the Anaheim Mental Health Agency in Anaheim. She would talk for about ten minutes to her busy case worker. Many times she could not see her psychiatrist and so we would have to make yet another appointment. When we could see the doctor I would sit with her when she went into the office to talk. Appointments at the Orange County Mental Health Agency were often rescheduled at their request. They would call our home and ask to speak to Kristin. I repeatedly told the office staff that she did not live with us and that she lived in a board and care facility they recommended. When I told them that I drove her to the appointment and they could tell me when the appointment was scheduled, they insisted on talking to Kristin reminding me of the privacy issue. I wanted to scream. Kristin had signed the papers making it legal for us to look at her records but still they would not tell us when her appointment was scheduled. I often asked myself, "Who's crazy now?"

We continued to follow the recommendations and requirements of the mental health center for a year and a half. Despite our many visits, Kristin was rarely called by her own name. Instead of making things better, the mental health system often added to the chaos of those it served. For example, in a five month period of treatment at Mental Health, Kristin saw five different psychiatrists. Doctor's appointments would have been funny if they had not been so tragic. Each appointment she was met by a different doctor sitting across the desk from her asking her to tell her story. She would turn to me with an expression of total exhaustion and begin going over the same information she told the last doctor. As Kristin began her story the doctor invariably reached for his prescription pad to renew the same medications perpetuating the same treatment plan. We were witnessing assembly line psychiatry.

Each time Kristin was asked to leave a residence I could see the disappointment in her eyes. She usually liked the house and the people there and so I couldn't figure out why she would jeopardize her living arrangement by breaking their simple rules. I blamed it on the Schizophrenia diagnosis she had been given years previous. After failing yet again to obey the house rules, Kristin's case worker was running out of housing options. As the very last resort, the case manager showed us the Royal Health Care facility. There were seventy clients residing in an older apartment building that had been converted for the residential care of the mentally ill. Driving up to the facility, my heart sank. Old and infirmed mental patients sat on hard benches smoking and talking to themselves. Others were lying in the parking lot outside the center. Most everyone had dazed looks on their faces.

The inside of the facility did not look any better than the outside. It was a two-story building with concrete floors and rooms off the hallways like a dormitory. I could not see Kristin improving in that nauseating living environment. After we turned down the case worker's suggestion she told us that she was completely out of ideas. She seemed irritated at having no other options to show us so we risked giving the Royal Health Care Facility a try. Kristin was not against the idea and said that she was willing to move there. Kristin settled into a dingy room in August of 2006. This was her eleventh move since coming to California. We wondered what move might be next because something told us that Kristin did not fit.

Every time we asked a question, we got another question. Both Kristin and our family moved into survival mode. Seeing the unpleasant state of Kristin's new surroundings caused me to wonder what I would think and how I would behave if I was asked to move every few weeks. There is a lonely feeling that sets in when you feel that you do not fit in. Sadly, there were times when Kristin was small when she told us that she just did not feel like she fit. Now as she bounced from facility to facility, her feelings were being validated. Despair crept into my mind and heart at night when all was quiet.

My husband and I joined the ranks of all concerned parents with a disabled child who ask, "What will become of my child?" The question that loomed before us was, "What would Kristin's future be?"

Chapter 10 The Missing Piece

Out of sheer desperation I began to think and dream about the kind of place where Kristin could live, learn and be herself in safety and comfort. I emailed about twenty well-connected friends expressing my dream of opening up a facility for adults with mental challenges. I envisioned a place where the needs of mentally disabled adults could to be met and their desires addressed. I saw a place where beauty and the worth of a disabled person would be honored. One day I received an email reply from Dr. Earl Henslin, a psychologist in Orange, California. He extended an invitation for me to join with him and his staff of counselors to brainstorm the perfect mental health facility. I was thrilled to accept his offer so off I went to the meeting. I sat in his office and gave our story of Kristin and how we wanted to open a place where her strengths could be recognized and her weaknesses improved. After the hour was up and the staff members went back to their offices, Dr. Henslin looked at me and asked me how I knew that Kristin had Schizophrenia. I recalled the long list of psychiatrists who had given their diagnoses. He just looked pensively at me. Then he asked if our daughter had ever had a brain scan. I said that she had gone through tests at Scripps Mercy Hospital, but that I had never really seen the results of those tests. I was awestruck when he told me that psychiatry was the only medical field where raw physiological data was not consistently used in diagnosing diseases. Opening my mind further he gave me this example: Imagine three people going to the doctor with pain in their arms and all three receiving different diagnoses and different medications without the benefit of an x-ray to prove that the diagnosis or treatment was correct. How can a doctor "see" inside the brain by merely listening to someone who is severely confused talk about their pain? How can that method be accurate one hundred percent of the time?

Psychiatrists usually talk to the patient and base their diagnosis on the conversations, behaviors and outward symptoms of the person. Medications are then dispensed after the diagnosis is determined. All this is done without actually looking at the organ that is broken or challenged. In other words, the brain is rarely looked at to make the diagnosis. How odd is that? And yet I had never really thought about it. After Kristin's first diagnosis of Schizophrenia on September 11, 2001 the doctors that followed merely repeated the same diagnosis without going any deeper into the cause. Dr. Henslin handed me a pamphlet about the Amen Clinic in Newport Beach. He told me about a technology called a SPECT (Single Photon Emission Computerized Tomography) scan that actually looks inside the brain. The benefit of the SPECT scan is that it shows the activity of a working brain. By measuring the flow of blood, the SPECT can uncover areas of over-activity or under-activity in the brain. Based on that evidence, a skilled doctor can more accurately decide what medications are necessary to balance the brain's chemistry.

I phoned the clinic and made an appointment for Kristin to be SPECT scanned. Jerry and I took her there and waited in the waiting room. Kristin craved a cigarette yet she was not supposed to smoke for 12 hours before the scan. By the time we got her to the clinic she was so nervous and anxious that she could barely sit still. The technician came to get her to take her in for the scan. After nearly 45 minutes, the technician came out and looked rumpled and tired. He asked if I would come in and talk to Kristin and keep her quiet and still because the scan was not readable. I walked back to the scanning room and helped her into position. With her head taped down to the table, the machine automatically pulled her back into the photographic tunnel. I calmly talked to her and counted down the minutes with her and softly held her chin motionless. I reminded her about how brave she was and how proud we were of her. I promised her that Dad would be standing at the door when it was all over with a fresh pack of cigarettes. In that moment those noxious cigarettes were no longer an issue with us. We had much bigger issues to deal with. Cigarettes had become a kind of currency with Kristin and they had also become Kristin's friends. Finally the scan was over and we walked out to the fresh air wondering what the test would show.

After a couple of weeks, we headed back to Newport Beach to the Amen Clinic to consult with a psychiatrist regarding Kristin's scan results. We were ushered into an office and waited as Dr. Todd Clements sat down at his desk and turned toward Kristin with a file in his hand. He asked Kristin if she had been told before that she had Schizophrenia and she nodded and said, "Yes." He pulled out another file and held up a SPECT brain image report and explained how that this person definitely had Schizophrenia and yet how different Kristin's scan looked in comparison. The SPECT images were radically different! He went on to say that he was positive that Kristin was NOT schizophrenic because the scan accurately showed that she did not have that disease. Kristin sort of shrugged and looked somewhat disinterested. Jerry and I were speechless. What was he saying? If she didn't have Schizophrenia, what then was Kristin's diagnosis? He went on to describe how that the scan clearly showed two symmetrical gashes in the frontal lobes of her brain. Also, there was evidence of a possible broken jaw in alignment with one side of her brain injury. He asked if she had been in an accident to cause such a severe brain injury.

My stomach turned and my face went numb. Kristin's thirty-one years flashed before my eyes and I instantly knew what had happened. Was a missing puzzle piece falling into place? I retold the story of being overdosed on Pitocin in 1975 and how the angry doctor came into my room and went into an emergency mode of shouting orders and ripping the I. V. drip from my arm. I could hear the doctor's words of "She's in distress" echoing in my mind. It made sense that the rushed manner in how the forceps were used would have caused the red marks on her head and injury to her brain. The facts began to come to us in rapid fire as we remembered her difficult birth. She was in intense pain and we couldn't figure out what was hurting her. She could only suckle on one side and would scream in pain if I tried to lay her on the opposite side. Could it be that her jaw was broken and she was unable to tell us of her pain? Her intense nasal infections and ear infections and even her lazy eye all seemed to have a connection to the diagnosis of traumatic brain injury. Her inability to process cause and effect and her lack of logic all pointed to the frontal lobe injury. The missing piece had been found! It was a strange feeling. Kristin had been living with a traumatic brain injury for 31 years! We sat there for quite some time in Dr. Clements' office just digesting the truth and allowing that truth to settle into our hearts and fill in the missing piece of information that we wondered about for so long. It had been a long and dangerous journey and yet we both realized on that day that we were finally on the right road.

Two things became very clear to us. We believed that Kristin was brain-injured by accident. We believe that God had a purpose for this accident in Kristin's life. We have mixed feelings about these insights. When I discovered that brain injury had been what was wrong all that time with Kristin, all I could think about was the years of wasted effort, wasted energy and all the mistakes. So many people had hurt her in ignorance of her condition. She wasn't just a rebellious child, wild teenager, or a confused young adult. Kristin was a strong woman. She had been fighting for her own survival for her entire life.

For the very first time in her life on that day in Dr. Clements' office, the function of Kristin's brain had been looked at, evaluated, properly diagnosed and respected for the limits it had. We were given a plan that accounted for the limited functions Kristin's brain could perform. It was a plan of action that was entirely different than plans she had grown used to for years. This plan was based on medical fact not speculation. Jerry and I wondered how we were going to pay for this plan. None of the treatments available at the Amen Clinics were covered by our insurance or state funding. We had relied on tax-supported care from county mental health programs for many years. We looked at one another and instinctively knew what our decision needed to be. We would not continue getting free care that was a combination of misdiagnosis and abuse. We were not crazy and Kristin was not crazy. The system was crazy in not adequately diagnosing and treating Kristin's disability. We called an end to the craziness that day and closed Kristin's file at Orange County Mental

Health. Now we were stepping determinedly into the next phase of the journey not knowing how we would cover the cost.

I wish I could tell you that all went smoothly from that day forward. It did not. The journey of the brain -injured is one of rough transitions, misunderstandings, and unawareness from the world at large. Now, after Kristin's new diagnosis, our resources have dwindled. We have no publicly-paid caseworkers and our psychiatrist, who is skilled to understand and treat patients based on a SPECT, requires a significant financial commitment. Office visits run on a schedule without cancellations. Treatments call for an intense investment of time and effort, as well. All of the heavy psychotropic medications prescribed by the county Mental Health department have been slowly changed. With new medication suited to balance her brain chemistry Kristin has awakened to become more the person she truly is.

In the year since receiving the new prescription plan based on the SPECT scan, we have seen dramatic results. Kristin no longer lives in a near comatose state with no energy or will to do anything. She is no longer overweight or chronically depressed. Kristin can still be argumentative or disruptive yet Kristin is a beautiful young woman in the making. It is a full-time job to monitor and resource her as she awakens to her own injury. Kristin's treatment plan remains flexible in order to help her through the changes that her body and mind require.

Understanding Kristin's inability to plan ahead has allowed us to connect with her in more efficient ways. We give her only what is needed for short term rather than expecting her to understand the consequences of waste. A week's supply of shampoo, conditioner, soap and batteries are now always readily available in our car for her. We buy inexpensive clothes for her and overlook the issue of her throwing out her belongings. We bring her surprises rather than wait for her to want to shop for items. She is still obsessive about certain things and often turns angry and frustrated if she is unable to obtain them. It is often like taking a spoiled toddler to a toy store and being bullied until you break down and buy what she is demanding. She has very little ability to restrain herself in a public setting. Without the appropriate brain inhibitor capacity, Kristin is apt to be socially inappropriate. Once when I was helping her do her laundry at a laundromat, we had a conflict. I had to hastily explain her disability to the operator because she had spoken out in a harsh and spiteful manner nearly causing a calamity. On another occasion when I was pumping gas at the station, Kristin's inability to make stable decisions almost caused a potentially dangerous situation. Kristin began to light up a cigarette right by the gas pump and another customer seeing the danger started yelling obscenities asking her if she was that dumb to do such a thing. Kristin looked bewildered and confused as she put out her cigarette and climbed into the front seat. I apologized and explained the action to the angry man. Later I attempted to explain the danger to Kristin as we drove off. These examples only touch on the difficult and intricate care we must give to Kristin now that we know she is the victim of a traumatic brain injury that happened at birth. Hard...yes. Important...Yes! Kristin is well worth it.

Over the last three years of care for Kristin, someone in the family often looked at another member and said, "Who's crazy now?" Sometimes it is the health care system that is crazy. Sometimes it is the health provider. Sometimes the school system or the criminal justice system appears to be crazy. When we lose our focus and respond to Kristin's behavior, rather than her disability, we can be crazy too. A brain injury in a family will turn your world upside down.

In 2008 we began a process to get some additional help for Kristin through a public resource tasked with helping the disabled. We discovered that gaining admittance to public programs for someone with traumatic brain injury is next to impossible. We learned that when we applied for Kristin to gain admittance into the Regional Center of California. The Regional Center is connected with the California Department of Disabilities and by law resources any state citizen who has been disabled before the age of eighteen. The Regional Center gives resources to those with disabilities by providing living arrangements and day programs. Entrance into the Regional Center is very important for families who have a disabled child. Many disabled people have found help but those with traumatic brain injury are not easily admitted.

To qualify for the Regional Center we needed to show proof of Kristin's disability. Unfortunately Kristin was misdiagnosed for years by professionals who were not familiar with the latest technological advances for proper diagnosis. We scoured Kristin's records for documented evidence in order to demonstrate to the Regional Center panel that Kristin was disabled at birth. Regrettably, her hospital records have been shredded. As a school child, Kristin did not attend special education classes because they were largely unavailable. To make up for her brain deficit, Jerry and I helped her with school assignments. Even with our help, Kristin barely got through school. Ignorant of her brain injury, we functioned for her and became her frontal lobes while she lived at home. Despite our gut intuitions, we initially believed the "experts" when they said that our daughter was normal. Sadly, we also believed the "experts" when they said that she was schizophrenic. Both misdiagnoses sent us on a long and treacherous path that did not offer Kristin the help she needed.

Though we presented the Orange County Regional center with extensive evidence from the American Psychiatric Association that gives the SPECT Scan veracity in diagnosing brain injures, we came up against strong negative reactions from their doctors. The testimony from a SPECT scan, a variety of other tests and the conclusions of medical doctors, a neuropsychologist and our psychiatrist, Dr. Todd Clements, was deemed insufficient. The county medical assessors insisted that Kristin was quite simply severely mentally ill and in need of a program of heavy psychotropic medications prescribed by Mental Health. Their solution painted a future as devastating as Kristin's past. We were told to send Kristin back to the County Mental Health system that failed her. We were told to listen to the same doctors who gave Kristin the wrong medications that turned our daughter comatose, robotic and damaged her heart and liver. We were told to send her back to the same doctors who never looked at her brain.

We couldn't help but think..."*Who's crazy now?*"

Who's Crazy Now?—Part 2
Todd Clements, M. D.

Chapter 11 The Reality of "Today"

Today in this country, the United States of America, something will happen —without fanfare and largely unnoticed. Over 2,500 people will sustain a brain injury. Almost 700 of these injuries will be moderate to severe. Over 500 people will be hospitalized today as a result of their brain injury. More than 100 of them will die in the next few weeks—many of them being kept alive only by machines.

More than 250 of these brain injury survivors will live with significant disabilities for the rest of their life as a result of the brain injury they experience today. Here again, without fanfare and largely unnoticed. Even though they do remain alive and here with us on earth, their lives are undoubtedly changed forever. These brain injuries happen in a matter of seconds and certainly aren't planned. Families aren't equipped or trained to deal with the emotional, medical, financial, and spiritual impact these injuries bring.

For many, a brain injury means dreams are lost and hopes are dashed. I think of Jerry Nadeau, an up and coming race car driver, in his early 30's, with NASCAR, who suffered a brain injury in a wreck at Richmond International Raceway on May 2, 2003. His racing career ended that day. I think of numerous patients I've seen whose heartbreaking brain injuries abruptly changed the whole course of their lives

Samantha was one of these. She was studying pre -med in college until flipping over the front handlebars of her bicycle. She never finished college (though she desperately tried for several years). Today she lives with her husband and her proudest accomplishment is that she learned to drive again (she drives a farm truck around the small town they live in).

Breanne was a champion gymnast until her brain injury. Now she is in and out of jail and has battled years of problems with addictions. Breanne's loving mother has spent untold thousands of dollars in caring for her. Since the brain injury Breanne spends much of the time angry and combative to her mother—her reasoning ability is very limited. Breanne's mother recently broke down in my office because she's so worried about what will happen to Breanne when she passes away.

Jason was captain of his high school football team as well as an all "A" student. Hopes were high for him receiving a scholarship from a top notch university—perhaps even an Ivy League school. A 70 foot fall from a local mountain during the summer between his junior and senior year dashed those dreams. Today, 10 years later, Jason lives with his parents and works odd jobs. He's made several attempts at junior college with no success. His life is riddled with extreme mood swings, irritability, and paranoia. There are times when he goes several days without sleeping—often due to paranoia. During these times he hears strange voices talking to him and experiences vivid visions.

Jason's parents, Tom and Lisa, are the ones who suffer the most. While he is content hanging out at home and watching TV most of the day—they are the ones who realize what could have been. Jason's main concern is that he doesn't have a girlfriend. Tom and Lisa know that he's too unstable for any girl in her right mind to date him. They also worry about Jason's future and bemoan the fact that he doesn't.

Will Jason have to live with us for the rest of our

lives? What will happen to him when we're too old to take care of him? Where will he go when we're gone? These are questions they never expected to ask. After all, Jason was the pride of their small town. With his talents and gifts he was surely headed for success.

Kristin's Traumatic Brain Injury

Kristin's brain injury happened at birth. Because of this we'll never really know what her life would have been like without it. One can only imagine.

I could tell you many more stories like these. Sadly, there are thousands (if not hundreds of thousands) of brain-injured in our country today. Thousands have returned from the battlefields of Iraq and Afghanistan with life changing brain injuries. The most recent statistics I've read estimated the number of brain-injured soldiers to be around 300,000 by the time our troops leave Iraq. Rather than turning the page to the next phase of life after the war, many of these young men and women will be forever challenged with overcoming the brain insult they now struggle with daily. Many of them too will be challenged with overcoming the government and medical community who often try to deny that they even have an injury.

Why is a Brain Injury So Traumatic?

What is the difference between me and Bill Gates? About fifty billion dollars may be the first answer that pops into your mind, and that is the essence of my question. Our brains are different. His brain has the amazing intelligence to understand intricate details about computer programs, allowing him to create computer software that has changed our lives. My brain has figured out how to turn on a computer and find my email. Anything much more complicated than that is going to require some assistance. But, there are probably some areas in life in which my brain is better than Bill Gates' (at least I'd like to think so).

Many factors contribute to who we are, but none are as strong an influencer as what I call the 3 B's (Brains, Brawn, and Blessings). As our society increases in technology, brains are becoming much more important than brawn (physical strength). Our brainpower plays a huge role in how we live. While our brain is the foundation of our intelligence, it is also the center of our personality. Your brain not only determines what you are, but who you are as well.

Phineas Gage

The strange story of Phineas Gage demonstrates one of the first discoveries revealing the power of our brains. Mr. Gage's tragic tale begins around 4:30pm on September, 13, 1848 in Vermont, where he worked as the foreman of a railway construction gang. Phineas was a success story already, at the young age of 26. His intelligence, athletic ability, and responsible caring personality all propelled him to a position of notable leadership in the railroad company. His bosses declared that he was the most efficient and capable man in their employ.

While preparing the landscape for future railroad tracks, which consisted of dynamiting large rocks, a terrible accident occurred. An unexpected explosion thrust (at high speed) a three foot long iron tamping rod in Phineas Gage's hands up through his left cheek bone, through his brain, and out the top of his skull. The tamping rod landed over 300 feet away (a whole football field).

Phineas had a few convulsions after he was thrown to the ground, but within a few minutes he was alert and rationally talking to his co-workers. Amazingly, he had somehow survived—even with a huge hole in his skull. Doctors watched him closely for the next several weeks expecting him to die (most likely from infection), but strangely he didn't. Two months later his doctors announced him cured—but was he?

One physician reported that Gage was fortunate because he injured an area of his brain that was expendable. However, Gage's friends and co-workers noted that his personality underwent such a dramatic change that they now barely recognized him.

This once polite and caring person resorted to frequent outbursts of profanity and aggression. His behavior was abhorrently selfish. He lied continually. He was erratic, unreliable, and couldn't follow through with any type of plan. His social graces were so poor that one of his doctors compared his behavior to that of an animal.

Even though Phineas Gage survived the physical brain injury from his accident he never recovered. His character remained changed forever. This change was so radical that his friends declared that, "Gage, was no longer Gage." His brain injury altered the very essence of who he was.

Phineas Gage had sustained damage to the frontal lobe of his brain. When one of his physicians wrote a paper on this in 1868 other doctors began noticing that their patients with frontal lobe injuries often experienced radical personality changes—similar to Phineas Gage. They couldn't hold a job, due to unreliability. They had little respect for social conventions and seemed indifferent to other people. Their lives usually crumbled around them as they were unable to execute and carry out any plans and they often made stupid decisions against their own best interests. Yes, doctors were beginning to understand that the brain may do more than direct the movement of the arms and legs (the conventional wisdom of that era).

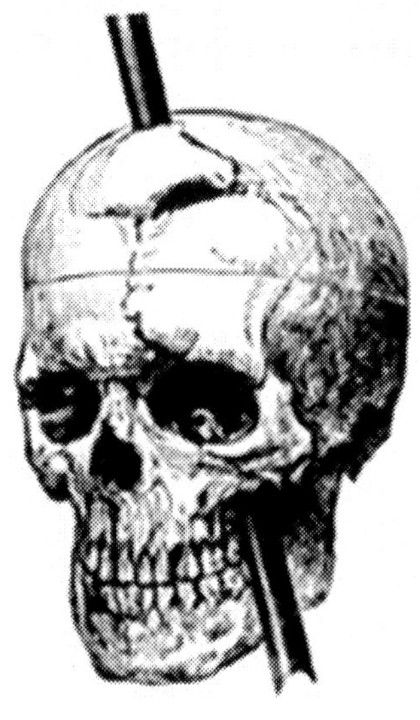

Phineas Gage's Skull

The Story of Henry M.

Henry M. was a very intelligent and friendly young man who lived a pleasant childhood in Connecticut. Henry experienced his first of many grand mal seizures on his sixteenth birthday. (The seizures were thought to be brought on by a head injury from an earlier bicycle accident.) The grand mal seizures continued, increasing in frequency and duration over the next ten years.

Unable to live alone or even hold a job, due to his frequent blackouts from the seizures, Henry's future looked bleak. After all, there was little that could be done for epilepsy back in those days. However, in 1953, at the age of 27, Henry entered the hospital full of hope. A new radical brain surgery, which removed sections of the temporal lobes, was supposed to cure his epilepsy.

The good news is that the surgery did improve his epilepsy. The bad news is that in removing a chunk of his right and left temporal lobes Henry was left stuck in 1953. He could not store any new memories. Henry could remember most everything that happened when he was a child, but he could only keep a new memory for about 30 seconds. He could not convert a short-term memory (e.g. learning someone's name) into a long-term memory (a process called consolidation). When he was older he could not even recognize his own face in a mirror.

Every morning was a completely new day for Henry. His doctors had to reintroduce themselves every time they walked into his room. Yes, this unintentional brain insult changed Henry's life forever. He has never been able make friends, marry, or live alone. He spent the rest of his years in a nursing home and experienced traumatic shock and grief each time he asked to visit his mother and was told (for the first time in his mind) that she had passed away.
Thankfully, the grief would only last for about 30 seconds and Henry would then forget what he was crying about.

The Most Important Organ?

Yes, without a doubt, our brain is the most important organ in our body and also the most complicated organ--it controls how we think, feel, and act. So when our brain works right we work right, but when it doesn't we're going to have trouble—trouble with our thinking, our feelings (emotions), and our behaviors—perhaps big trouble. Brain injuries affect us both physically and mentally. They affect our intelligence, our ability to learn, and even our common sense.

Thinking

How many thoughts pass through your mind a day—hundreds, thousands, perhaps tens of thousands? Thoughts are created in the brain and even stored there as memories. Our thoughts enable us to make decisions, learn a new task, solve a problem, and remember the name of someone we meet. It would be impossible to function without thoughts. Our thoughts even allow us the ability to reason, recall detailed events from the past, and contemplate the future. These superior abilities of our brain separate us from any other animal on the earth. Indeed our brains are so developed that we are the only living creatures who can see into the future and realize that we will surely die one day.

Brain injuries limit our ability to create, organize, and store our thoughts. People with brain injuries experience more difficulty organizing thoughts, keeping their attention focused, and planning out and following through with tasks. This can run the gamut from minor memory and decision making deficits to the total loss of the ability to reason or think abstractly.

The thinking (or reasoning) part of our brain is often referred to as the mind, which to some is a separate entity from the brain. While the brain does indeed do more than just think, the two cannot be separated out. Whatever affects our brain will affect our mind. An injury to the brain will result in changes to the way we think. A small injury may result in only subtle changes, but any insult to the brain matters.

Feelings

Feelings come from the brain!

The revelation in the prior section about our brain controlling our thoughts is about as surprising as finding out that Dolly Parton has had plastic surgery. Most of us know very well of the brain-thinking connection. However, the brain-feelings connection is often overlooked. Feelings do not come from the heart as many suppose, but rather the brain.

Feelings are what we feel on the inside. They are very subjective and difficult to control. Emotions are what we show on the outside. I might feel fearful on the inside, but could show no emotion, or another emotion, such as anger. Our feelings, along with the thoughts about those feelings, determine our emotions. Brain injury affects both feelings and emotions. People with brain injuries report more problems with depression, mood swings, anxiety, and suicidal thoughts when compared to the general public.

People with brain injuries are often perceived to be mentally ill. The peculiar behavior of billionaire Howard Hughes has been well noted. Some of his family members have noted that his behavior became strange and erratic after a plane crash in 1946 that landed him in the hospital for several weeks. He likely suffered undiagnosed brain injury from that crash (the means to assess for brain injury at that time was very limited).

I can understand a brain injury being overlooked 70 years ago, but the sad fact is that it's still happening at an alarming rate today. It took over 30 years to recognize Kristin's brain injury. But she's just a small scrape off the tip of the iceberg.

Over 100 an hour

We're not talking about miles here, but rather the number of people in this country who sustain a brain injury. Yes, that's right—on average more than 100 people an hour in this country joins the ranks of the brain injured. This may even be underestimating it—one popular documentary on brain injury titled

"Every 21 Seconds" reports that as the frequency of new brain injuries in this country.

Each year in the United States:

- Over 1 million people are treated for brain injuries in hospital emergency rooms
- Over 250,000 people suffer a moderate or severe brain injury
- Over 50,000 people die from their brain injuries
- Over 200,000 are hospitalized, but survive
- Over 50,000 suffer seizures from the brain injury
- Over 100,000 of the survivors live with significant disabilities from their brain injury

Over 5 million people in the United States today are living with a brain injury

Who Are These People?

We often hear when a famous person, such as Bob Woodruff, the ABC news anchor, sustains a brain injury. The good news about this is that he has used his time, resources, and talent to educate the public about brain injuries. We also often hear the news about successful people who overcame a brain injury. I think of Norman Brinker here, the wealthy restaurateur, who sustained a brain injury playing polo in 1993. His brain injury put him in a coma and nearly killed him, but he worked hard in rehab and came back from it. But by and large, the vast majority of the millions of brain injured people alive today are not well known people. Some are barely known outside their family circle. The struggles and hardships they endure everyday are rarely known either.

Any person at any age can suffer a brain trauma at anytime (yes, even while you're sleeping). It often happens unexpectedly—and in the blink of a second—catching everyone off guard. Let's look at who these people are.

Young Males

Three out of four new brain injuries involve males. Young males aged 15-24 are the most vulnerable group. Largely because they are the highest "risk takers" in our society. The majority of brain injuries in this group occurs from accidents—particularly traffic accidents with automobiles and motorcycles. Vehicle crashes are the most common cause of brain injury for anyone under the age of 65. One-third of these accidents involve alcohol or drugs. Brain injuries beget brain injuries, as one-third of those who go to the Emergency Room with a brain injury have been there before. Being single also increases a male's chances of suffering a brain injury—so yes; having a wife can save your brain.

Young males also make up the largest portion of the military (including the soldiers returning from Iraq). An estimated one out of five soldiers returning home from the war is dealing with some degree of brain injury. Traumatic Brain Injury has been referred to as the signature injury among soldiers in the Iraq war.

Young males are also the most likely group to sustain a brain injury from sports. The heavy contact sports such as boxing, football, and rugby come to mind first—and indeed they should. However, other sports traditionally considered non-contact have their share of brain injuries as well.

- Soccer—heading the ball can cause a concussion injury to the brain, but the most severe injuries occur when players bang heads together.
- Skiing—both water and snow skiing (and snowboarding)
- Wrestling—both the real and fake kind (wrasslin')
- Biking—the largest source of sports related injury in children—especially when not wearing a helmet.

Elderly

The elderly are the second highest risk group for brain injuries. Falls are the most common source of brain injury for people who are 65 and older. Falls can lead to death—often from brain bleeding (which is especially a problem with elderly people who take blood thinners) and from brain swelling. But, only one out of nine people will die from their fall. The remaining eight will survive--with the brain injury.

Other Causes

Birth trauma, as in Kristin's case, is another cause of brain injury. Using forceps in a delivery increases the risk.

Violence unfortunately is a significant cause of brain injury in this country. The victims are frequently women battered by domestic abusers, and innocent children. Firearms are also involved in traumatic brain injuries. Almost two-thirds of brain injuries from firearms stem from a suicide attempt.

Chapter 12 What does a Brain Injury Look Like?

Finding a brain injury can be quite tricky. You cannot see the brain as it is completely covered by solid bone. Sometimes the symptoms of a brain injury are evident immediately, but often the changes don't surface until days, weeks, or months after an injury. Contrary to popular notion, getting knocked out (loss of consciousness) or how long you were knocked out, is a poor predictor of the presence or severity of a brain injury. Loss of consciousness is more dependent on the area of the brain affected rather than the severity of the injury. Yes, you can have a severe brain injury and never lose consciousness—Phineas Gage did. Here are some signs and symptoms that often occur with brain injury:

Mild Brain Injury

- The patient may remain conscious or lose it for a few seconds or minutes
- The person may feel dazed or not like himself for weeks after the injury
- Frequent headaches
- Confusion, change in memory, problems with concentration
- Lightheadedness, dizziness, blurred vision, double vision
- Tinnitus (ringing in the ears)
- An unusual taste in the mouth
- Daily fatigue
- A change in sleep patterns (may sleep too much or

may not be able to go to sleep)
- Mood and behavior changes

Moderate/Severe Brain Injury

- There may or may not be loss of consciousness
- Persistent headache—may worsen over time
- Dilated pupils (may affect one or both pupils)
- Nausea and vomiting
- Seizures
- Loss of balance, weakness in the legs or arms
- Slurred or slow speech
- Confusion, amnesia for events that happened several hours to days after the injury
- Inability to waken after falling asleep
- Restlessness, agitation

Note: Small children or infants who experience a brain injury may show some of the above symptoms as well as these:

- Continual crying with the inability to be consoled
- Refusal to nurse or eat

Types of Brain Injury

Acquired Brain Injuries (ABI) are divided into Traumatic Brain Injury (TBI) or non-Traumatic Brain Injury (NTBI) The trauma can be localized to one area of the brain (focal) or involve several brain regions (diffuse).

Brain cells are called neurons as pictured below. They consist of an axon (A), dendrites (B), and a cell body with a nucleus (C). Some neurons exist specifically to nourish and protect other neurons. However, injury to any type of neuron interferes with brain functioning.

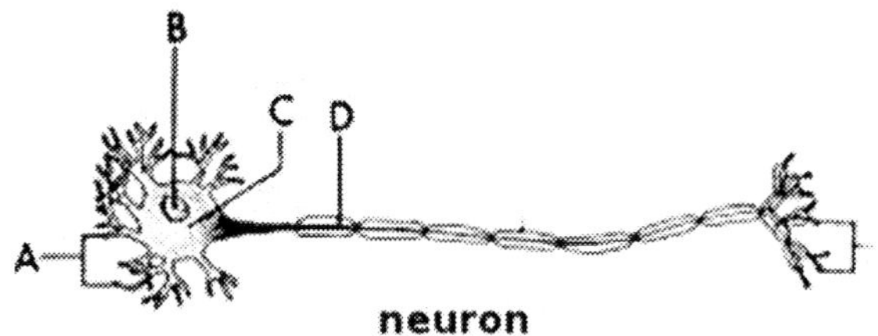

A. dendrites B. nuceus c. cell body

Terms that describe the ways brain cells are injured:

Concussion

Concussion happens when a blow or jolt to the head causes your brain to bounce against the inner walls of your skull. This causes temporary changes that interfere with the brain's functioning. These changes lead to chemical imbalances inside the brain cells and also may reduce blood flow to the brain. Basically, a concussion doesn't usually kill brain cells, but instead makes them sick and temporarily malfunctioning.

The main symptoms at the time of a concussion are headaches and amnesia surrounding the event. Most of the time people do not lose consciousness, but they may not be able to remember the concussion happening. I've treated football and soccer players who have received concussions during a sporting event who were unable to remember even playing a game that day. They were never knocked out and some of them even stayed in the game!

Next, symptoms such as memory problems, confusion, crankiness, inability to control emotions, and loss of interest may appear. Concussion symptoms are not life threatening and they usually subside on their own in several weeks. Occasionally they may continue on for several months in what's called a post

-concussive syndrome.

More than a million concussions occur in this country each year. "Concussion" is an older term and today "minor head trauma" or "mild traumatic brain injury (MTBI) are more correct terms. These are often used interchangeably.

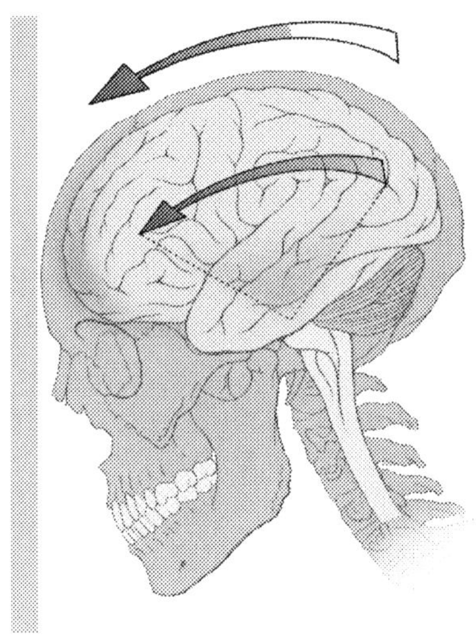

Concussion

Contusion

A contusion is a bruising of brain tissue. This happens when small vessels are injured and leak blood into brain tissue. These primarily occur in areas of the brain located near sharp ridges on the inside of the skull. Many people are surprised to find out that the inside of the skull is quite different from the smooth outside. The inner skull contains cavities and sharp bony ridges, which play a significant role in brain injury. Contusions usually heal on their own without medical intervention. However, there is the chance of edema (brain swelling) which can increase the pressure inside the skull and possibly lead to a coma.

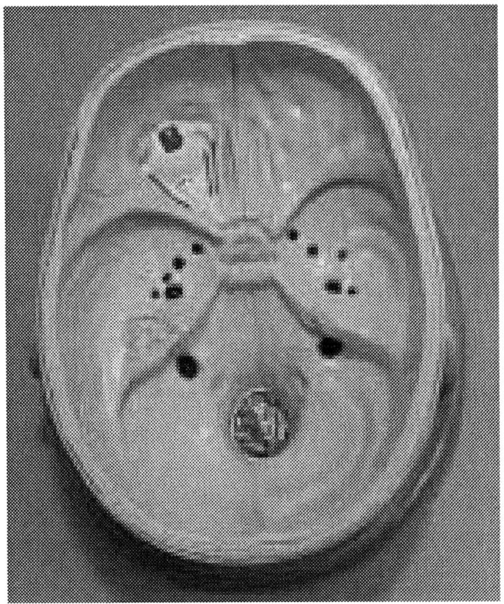

Inside of the Skull

Intracranial hemorrhage

Intracranial hemorrhage is bleeding within the skull. This occurs when a blood vessel in the head is ruptured (a much bigger blood vessel than a contusion). These are serious medical emergencies as the buildup of blood within the skull can increase the internal pressure, which can lead to a coma or death. Intracranial hemorrhages can be caused by trauma or non-traumatic causes such as strokes or aneurysms. Taking blood thinners increases the risk of brain hemorrhaging.

Diffuse Axonal Injury

This is one of the most devastating types of brain injury, which occurs in about one-half of all brain injuries. Damage is caused when axons are stretched and torn. This results when the head is rapidly accelerated or decelerated (motor vehicle accidents, shaken baby syndrome). It rarely kills a person, but is a frequent cause of coma or a persistent vegetative state. The frontal and temporal lobes are the most likely parts of the brain to sustain this type of injury.

Diffuse axonal injury has two parts: a primary injury—the initial axon damage resulting directly from the force—and then the secondary injury—a poorly understood process where stretched axon initially survive the trauma, but then biochemical changes occur inside the neuron and it dies over the next several days.

Anoxic Injury

Brain cells are damaged from a partial (hypoxic) or a complete (anoxic) lack of oxygen. Brain cells without oxygen start to die in only a few minutes. In fact, unconsciousness can occur in 15 seconds and irreversible brain damage in 5 minutes of oxygen deprivation. Serious brain injury can happen from kids using the "sleeper hold" in wrestling on each other. Newborns are also vulnerable to anoxic injuries.

There are 3 types of anoxic injuries:

- *Anoxic anoxia*—no oxygen from the lack of blood flow. The most common causes are heart attacks, strokes, and injuries with substantial blood loss.
- *Anemic anoxia*—the blood doesn't carry enough oxygen. Can happen from severe anemia, carbon monoxide poisoning, drowning, asphyxia, and suicide attempts.
- *Toxic anoxia*—toxins block oxygen in the blood from being used. The most common causes are infections and encephalitis.

The frontal lobe is the most vulnerable area of the brain to anoxia or hypoxia.

Coup-Contrecoup

This traumatic brain injury results when two injuries occur from one blow. The coup injury occurs under the site of impact. The contrecoup injury occurs on the side opposite the area that was impacted. This is caused by the brain bouncing back and forth against the skull. Vehicle accidents frequently cause coup-contrecoup injuries. You can also sustain a coup -contrecoup injury without direct impact to the head, such as with a whiplash or shaken baby syndrome.

Penetrating Brain Injury

This injury is a tearing of the brain from a skull fracture or gunshot wound. It causes large vessels to rupture and bleed into the brain and the space between the brain and skull. These types of injuries also allow bacteria into the brain, which can lead to infections such as encephalitis and meningitis.

Fearfully and Wonderfully Made

The human brain weighs a mere three pounds—about 2% of our average body weight. But this three pound mass, comprised largely of water and fat tissue, can make a thousand pound super computer look like child's play. In fact, it was the three pound brain that invented the supercomputer to start with! We truly are wonderfully and fearfully made.

Inside these three pounds live over 100 billion neurons. Each neuron can communicate with thousands of other neurons—some estimate that a brain cell can connect to at least 40 thousand other brain cells. Our understanding of how these living cells communicate with each other and work together to perform tasks is infinitesimal. But, the encouraging news is that our knowledge is increasing every day.

The human brain is divided into several different

areas, or lobes. In traumatic brain injury the damage may be confined to a specific location in the brain, or it may be diffuse, affecting many different parts of the brain. This is what makes the symptoms and treatment of brain injuries so indefinite and unique for each person. No two brain injuries are the exact same—just as no two brains are the exact same.

We do have some understanding of what functions each brain area controls. This allows us to make guesses about the nature of the problems an individual may have from knowing the location of a brain injury. We can also learn a lot about someone's brain injury by observing him in his day to day activities. Every activity we perform—mental or physical—are directed by certain parts of our brain.

We're going to look at the different lobes of our brain to better understand their functioning, but please understand that the brain functions as a whole, as the different lobes communicate and interrelate with each other. An injury may only disrupt a particular step of an activity occurring in the brain, but that out of sequence step can alter the whole process.

Is Bigger Better?

Humans are the most intelligent creatures on the earth (though it may not appear so if you spend an afternoon hanging out at the mall). Yet we don't have the biggest sized brain in the animal kingdom. Elephants brains can weigh over 12 pounds and a humpback whale may have a brain six times the size of a human one (at least we have the ant beat—their brains are 1/100 of a gram—merely a speck). But we're smarter than elephants and whales. Two factors play a huge role here—the size of our brain compared to the rest of our body and the percentage of our frontal lobes that make up our brain. So bigger is not necessarily better.

Chapter 13 The Frontal Lobe- Our CEO

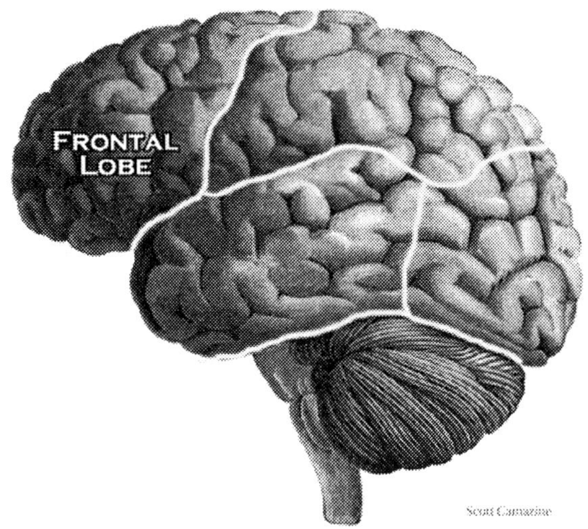

In humans the frontal lobes make up roughly 33% of our brain. The closest animal to us is the chimpanzee with 16% frontal lobe. Dogs have around 7% frontal lobes, while a domestic cat only has about 4%. The frontal lobes allow us to do things that separate us from all other animals, such as reason, plan for the future, exhibit empathy, and solve complex problems. Our frontal lobes are the last area of our brain to mature. In fact, they do not fully mature until our mid twenties. You'll see when we look at its specific functions how these are not usually present in small children, but develop gradually with training and aging.

The frontal lobes' large size makes them a very common area of injury—in fact, the most common in mild to moderate traumatic brain injury. They are home to our personality and emotional control. Injuries here can cause a wide variety of symptoms. Personality changes may range from very mild to so severe that friends and family may not even recognize the new personality.

The CEO

The front part of the frontal lobes is called the Prefrontal Cortex, or PFC. This area of the brain is often referred to as our center for executive functioning, or the CEO (Chief Executive Officer) of the brain. Executive functioning includes the ability to make sound decisions, to think abstractly, to organize, and to follow through with plans. People with problems in this area may exhibit short attention spans, leaving an inability to solve most types of complex problems. These people are often disorganized in getting tasks done, especially if the task involves several steps, and managing their time. I know a gentleman with a frontal lobe injury who has undertaken the task of writing a book about his experience in life with a head injury. He's been working on it for several years now, but has so far been unable to get organized enough to follow through on completing the project.

Impulse Control

The PFC helps determine our ability to control acting out on impulses. It allows us to exercise forethought—thinking before we say or act on whatever thought pops into our mind. Problems in this area can lead to socially unacceptable or dangerous behaviors. Think of children here who tend to say whatever comes to mind without considering the consequences (my mother used to call that putting your mouth in gear before engaging your brain).

Brain-injured people can show this same behavior. Others often have a hard time realizing that inappropriate remarks or behaviors from brain injured people are rarely done on purpose or maliciously, but rather because their frontal lobe doesn't filter correctly.

Donald, a man in his late 30's who had sustained a frontal lobe injury after crashing the small plane he owned and piloted, came into my office one afternoon for his appointment. One of the ladies working the front desk told him that he was over an hour late. Donald said that he had called the office earlier in the day saying that he wouldn't be able to make it on time and the person he spoke with told him to just come as soon as he could and that I could fit him in sometime that afternoon. When the receptionist asked him who he had spoken with (Donald knew all the office staff) a blank look came over his face then he said, "The fat ugly bitch who sits in that chair right there."

Thankfully, the lady whom Donald referred to had gone home early that day. The girls in the front were horrified by what he said (other patients in the waiting room also heard the exchange). When I asked Donald about it he simply said, "I didn't mean to say that. Do you want me to write her an apology?" And he was speaking the truth—this man didn't have a mean bone in his body. The Donald before the plane crash would have never said anything like that. But the way his brain worked now anything was liable to come out.

Impulsive behavior comes in many forms. It might be buying a beautiful piece of jewelry in a store window on a whim—when you really don't have the money (stores thrive of these types of people). Or it could be engaging in sexual activity with someone you just met. I've had patients impulsively shoplift items from a store when they had plenty of money to buy it.

Poor impulse control lead to irresponsible and unhealthy behaviors. These people often have trouble keeping their commitments in relationships, showing up to work on time. It's hard to be responsible when you're unable to stop yourself from acting out on impulsive thoughts running through your mind. These people also have increased rates of accidents, traffic tickets, and bodily injuries.

Living in the Present

People with impaired PFC functioning tend to live in the here and now as opposed to thinking of, planning for, or even caring about the future. They often rarely think about the past as well. There is a lack of putting cause and effect together (if I don't go to bed tonight I won't feel good tomorrow). This leads to poor judgment and the likelihood of making the same mistakes over and over, with little insight into these behavior patterns.

Tina, a young lady who received frontal lobe brain trauma from a snow sledding accident at 16 years old, moved into the dorm her freshman year of college. She had a high IQ and continued to make good grades after her accident. Her parents did notice a change in her personality and decision-making skills. They were strict though, and always made sure that her homework and chores were done. They were concerned about her living on campus at college, but decided to let her try it since they lived only about twenty minutes away from the campus and her roommate was Pam, a high school friend, whom they knew and trusted.

Several weeks into the semester Pam called Tina's mother worried about Tina, as she was staying up most of the night watching television and missing classes. Tina was fascinated with the program "The

Dog Whisperer." She would start watching the show around 10 pm and the network usually showed multiple episodes one after another. She wasn't getting to bed until 4 or 5 a.m. and then she was unable to get up for class. Many of the episodes were re-runs she had seen multiple times before.

Tina's TV watching spread to crime mysteries on Court TV—particularly the show "Forensic Files." Here again, she had seen them all and was watching many of them for the umpteenth time. If Tina felt like watching TV at midnight, that's what she did. If she had a test at 9am the next morning she didn't concern herself about that test until 9 a.m. This may seem like a no-stress way to live life, but the problem is that without the propensity to plan and work for the future not much gets accomplished.

Tina's parents (with her acceptance) finally took her TV to their house. But, sadly Tina had to withdraw from college. She moved back home and took classes at a junior college. She succeeded there because her parents stayed on top of her and made sure she completed her assignments (and turned off the TV at 10pm). They acted as her frontal lobes.

The Focus Factor

Our senses are constantly bombarded by stimuli when we're awake, though we're often unaware of this. Let me share just a minute in time with you of what I experienced last night.

"As I sat in Roy's restaurant I suddenly made note of everything my brain was attending to at that moment—there were two distinct conversations that I could hear at our table, there were other people talking around us. My eyes took notice of all the people that walked by—particularly our waiter. I also caught myself looking to see if I knew any of the people who sauntered past our table and

out of the corner of my eye I caught glimpses of the different football games playing on the various flat screen televisions in the restaurant.

I could smell the aroma of the fresh baked bread emanating out of the kitchen. I also caught whiffs of wonderful dishes passing by my table – headed to other patrons. Then last, but not least was the enriching smell from my own plate – along with five others at my table.

We sat near the door, so each time it opened I could feel the cool wet air of a rainy night as it made contact with my skin. Once the door closed I could sense the dry warmth from the propane heater stationed close by. As I took in all these happenings surrounding me, I still enjoyed the wonderful tastes of my own food and drink."

It's amazing how much information our brain has to take in and process at one time. Not only does it have to interpret what we're experiencing, but it also has to decide what is important and needs to be attended to and what can be relegated to the background. For instance, the monitoring of air temperature stays in the background, even though it's continually being monitored, until it drops to a certain point—and then it pops into the forefront and we notice that it's cold and take steps to warm up, such as putting on a jacket or moving close to the heater.

The prefrontal cortex plays a large role in our ability to properly focus. Especially an area known as Brodmann area 10. Abnormal functioning of this region can hijack this regulation. This results in jumping from stimulus to another—disorganization. Disorganization can range from minor inconveniences to problems in organizing your space—(room, house, office) to organizing your tasks (paying bills, homework, paperwork for job) to organizing your time (procrastination, not getting tasks accomplished, missing deadlines).

One of the hallmarks of ADD (Attention Deficit Disorder) is abnormal functioning of the prefrontal cortex. A properly functioning frontal lobe tells us what's most important and then helps us stay on task to complete it—even if it's not the most enjoyable thing we could be doing at that time. People with frontal lobe brain injury are very frequently diagnosed with attention deficit disorder.

Mad or Glad – Never Sad

Many people with frontal lobe injuries don't realize that they have any problems (they don't get it that they don't get it and they don't care). They are often indifferent to the wants and needs of others and may have little empathy (the capacity to understand someone else's state of mind). The frontal lobe has huge implications on our personality—just as we saw with Phineas Gage, whose brain injury localized to the frontal lobes.

Craig was in his early 30's when his family brought him in to be evaluated for memory problems. His brain scans showed significant injury, including an area in the right frontal lobe. When Craig was 17 he was thrown out of a go-cart going about 30 miles an hour and hit a tree. He lost consciousness for about 30 minutes and was in a daze for several days. Craig and his brother hid the news about the accident from their parents for a couple weeks so Craig never went to the doctor. Craig managed well after that, but his memory had never been the same.

When I asked Craig's family about his moods they shared with me that he'd always been a pretty happy-go-lucky guy, but since the accident they'd noticed that he didn't seem to experience the normal range of emotions. They explained how the family joke is that he has two moods—mad or glad. "He never shows sadness," his mother said, "Even when close family members have died. It's like he doesn't feel emotional pain, nor does he realize when we do. Even our friends have noticed this and he was a very sensitive child."

Craig's mother had asked his physician if Craig's personality could have changed as a result of the go-cart accident; and even though the doctor doubted it, the family felt strongly that it had changed. This same physician kept telling them Craig's memory was fine—when we tested him it was equivalent to someone in the early stages of dementia. The people who knew Craig best swore he was a different person after the go-cart incident.

While most of the time Craig was a friendly person who was enjoyable to be around, he was never able to develop empathy—the capability to understand another person's feelings or motives. He had very little insight into his own emotions. Learning about his frontal lobe was very helpful to his family, who now understood why he had never had a girlfriend—nor seemed interested in one.

Movement

The back part of the frontal lobe contains an area called the motor cortex, which controls the movement of body parts (this area lies just behind the prefrontal cortex). Injury in this area can result in loss of fine movements as well as loss of strength in the arms, hands, and fingers. These people may also exhibit very little spontaneous facial expression. People might report that they have a "Parkinsonian" look. People with Parkinson's disease often have blank facial expressions.

Injury to the motor cortex may mean having to learn all over how to walk again. Some people face the task of retraining their muscles in order to talk and communicate. Any task that requires muscle use and coordination may be affected by an injury to this area of the brain.

Broca's Area

Broca's area consists of a small part of the frontal lobe. This section is involved in language processing and speech. People suffering damage to this area may develop a condition known as Broca's Aphasia. They can understand what people are saying to them, but they have difficulty finding the right words to say. They may not be able to speak at all or when they try to speak their sentences may come out as disjointed words. They can say words, but have trouble putting them together in a meaningful way in sentences. In attempting to explain seeing a dog bite a man's hand they might say, "Dog uh yes, bit ah ah, man uh teeth, yes, see uh hand."

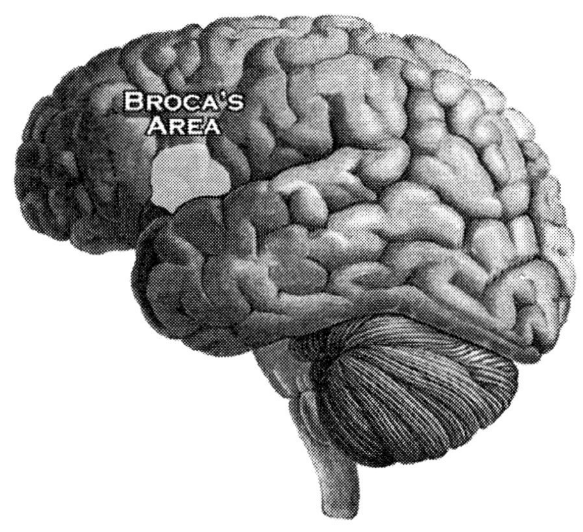

Personality Plus

The above examples merely touch the surface in examining the effects of the frontal lobes on our personalities. The aim of this book is not to provide an exhaustive review on every facet of brain injury, but to increase your awareness of just how encompassing a brain injury can be. Altering the functioning of the prefrontal cortex can alter the very essence of who you are. Here is a summary of frontal lobe functions and problems:

Frontal Lobe Functions

- Personality
- Focus
- Impulse control
- Organization
- Planning
- Time management
- Problem solving
- Critical thinking
- Forward thinking
- Perseverance
- Judgment
- Empathy
- Ability to feel and express emotions
- Insight
- Learning from mistakes
- Expressing language
- Movement of body parts (motor cortex)

Frontal Lobe Problems

- Personality Changes
- Short attention span
- Distractibility

- Disorganization
- Poor time management (chronic tardiness, procrastination)
- Impulse control problems
- Lack of perseverance
- Controlling emotions (mood changes)
- Lack of spontaneity in interacting with others
- Lack of empathy
- Poor judgment
- Trouble learning from experience
- Lack of insight into behavior
- Poor motivation
- Loss of movement or paralysis (motor cortex)
- Inability to express language (Broca's Area)

Chapter 14 Traveling Through the Brain

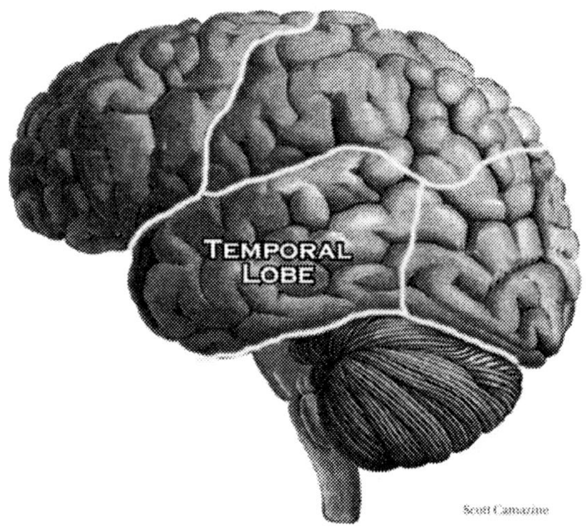

Temporal Lobes

The temporal lobes have often referred to in the past as merely the "armrests of the brain." Their functions have been historically shrouded in mystery, until recent years. Today, we know that the temporal lobes play a large role in our memory, learning, and emotional stability.

Unfortunately our temporal lobes are very prone to injury, primarily due to their location as well as the makeup of the inside of the skull. Our skulls are nice and smooth on the outside (you may have a little bumpiness and that's okay). But don't let the outside fool you—the inside is full of sharp bony ridges, as we saw above, particularly around the temporal lobes. When the brain shakes back and forth during an injury neurons and blood vessels in the temporal lobe area frequently tear and bleed, and the functioning of this area is compromised.

Language & Reading

For most people the dominant temporal lobe is the left side. The dominant temporal lobe allows us to understand language and have communication with each other. It enables you to understand the words you are reading in this book and put them together in a sentence. It has been well documented that abnormal left temporal lobe functioning often accompanies dyslexia (a learning disability in reading and spelling). People with no history of dyslexia who then experience a left temporal lobe injury have been known to have dyslexia afterwards.

Memory

Both temporal lobes are involved in processing, storing, and making memories. The dominant temporal lobe plays a large role in memory, which is one of the most important jobs of our brains. If your memory is not working right you won't fare well in life. The temporal lobes allow you to consolidate new memories into long term storage. Alzheimer's disease is a disease process in which there is progressive wasting of the temporal lobes, which leaves its sufferers unable to store new memories. Henry M., who we discussed earlier, had part of his temporal lobe removed and he could not form new memories. This forced him to move into a nursing home at a young age.

Amnesia, where people may be unable to remember all or periods of their past, is a consequence of temporal lobe malfunctioning. Memory problems may fluctuate as people with temporal lobe dysfunction experience periods when they tend to be more forgetful, but then during other times their memory may be fantastic.

Kristin's brain injury included her temporal and frontal lobes. Her memory deficiencies have caused grief for her and her family. Kristin has been asked to leave boarding homes and treatment facilities on numerous occasions for not complying with the rules. Kristin's rule-breaking was not intentional, but rather due to her inability to remember specific rules. Kristin's memory troubles keep her from having a job--unless someone was there to constantly remind her when to be at work, what she's supposed to do and what the rules are.

Before understanding how Kristin's brain worked, these types of behaviors drove her parents crazy. Her treatment facilities simply viewed these behaviors as rebellious and spiteful. Kristin's parents knew she was innocent of purposefully acting this way, but they couldn't fathom why she would sabotage all the hours of work they had spent in finding her room and board. Now they realize the role her brain injury plays in this behavior.

Aggression

Injury in the dominant temporal lobe can result in someone with a short fuse, who is prone to aggression. This aggression often stems from frustration—or rather, poor frustration tolerance. Once these people reach a certain level of frustration their response is usually to explode. Dr. Daniel Amen studied aggressive behavior in his clinic and found that almost three out of four people who had assaulted another person or damaged property in a fit of rage displayed left temporal lobe abnormalities. Laboratory studies have shown that when the amygdala, a small structure within the temporal lobes, is electrically stimulated in people they become aggressive and agitated.

These people will often describe their anger as an on and off switch. An event happens that turns on their anger button and they go into an immediate rage. They often feel remorse afterwards and may even apologize to anyone who was involved in the incident. But, while it's happening it's impossible to talk or reason with them

One lady told me how each morning she would get up and say to herself, "I'm going to go the whole day without losing my temper" but invariable some event would set her off. As she realized she was breaking her pledge she would try to stop herself, but the rage inside her was too intense to hold back.

Kristin exhibits classic signs of temporal lobe dysfunction when it comes to anger. She became infuriated at a family dinner one day and physically attacked Jerry trying to strangle him. Once Jerry calmed her down she went right back to normal—the switch had turned off as quickly as it turned on.

Aggression, while often expressed externally can also be expressed internally. When this happens people may try to harm themselves by self-injury, such as cutting, burning, or banging their heads on the wall. It may even lead to a suicide attempt or completion.

Tom

Tom, a college student, consulted with me at his parents' persistence after running into trouble with the law. A few months earlier he snuck into a nightclub with some of his college baseball teammates, while they were out of town playing in a tournament. He asked a girl to dance—who gladly accepted, but neglected to mention that her boyfriend was in the next room shooting pool. Tom only remembers seeing stars as he felt the forceful blow to his skull. He fell to the ground with sharp shooting pains on the left side of his head. The jealous boyfriend had walked up behind Tom and whacked him upside the head with a cue stick.

Tom's friends noticed a change in him during the next few months, particularly his issues with anger. There were several circumstances where Tom accused various teammates of talking about him or plotting against him. He was suspended from the team after he physically attacked a pitcher whom he thought was trying to hit him with the baseball.

Shortly after that incident Tom drove his car into the dealership to replace a burned out tail light. When Tom returned home and realized the tail light he had paid to replace wasn't working, he raced back up to the dealership. Outside the showroom he screamed obscenities and demanded the manager to come out. When this didn't happen immediately, Tom went ballistic slamming his fists repeatedly into one of their new cars.

The dealership called the police to arrest Tom. The manager finally did come out and told Tom he was sorry about the problems with his taillight and that it must have a short in it because it was working when Tom left the dealership. The manager offered to repair the electrical problems with the light for no charge and even throw in an oil change for Tom's trouble—but he did insist that Tom would have to pay for the damage to the showroom car or face criminal charges.

Everyone who knew Tom claimed his recent moodiness and tendency to fly off the handle was totally unlike him. Tom was frustrated by his behaviors as well and shared that he felt "mad and moody" most of the time now. When he had his brain scanned there was clear evidence of damage to his left temporal lobe.

Paranoia

Dysfunction in the dominant temporal lobe can result in sensitivity to slights, or mild paranoia. People who are paranoid experience excessive anxiety and fear that harm is going to occur to them. They usually think—irrationally--that others have bad intentions for them. Paul, an Iraqi war veteran who sustained a brain injury from an IED, claimed he had killed a young Iraqi man in hand to hand combat during an inner city firefight (I was never able to verify the accuracy of his claim). He was sure that the Iraqi man's family was now here in America searching to kill him and avenge their relative's death. Two years after returning home, Paul was still afraid to leave his house most days. When his family did persuade him to go into town with them he would flee anytime he saw someone who even slightly appeared to be of Arab descent.

Terry was another young man who sustained left temporal lobe damage--again from his service in the Iraq war. He constantly felt people were out to get him once he returned home. But rather than a specific person for a specific reason, like Paul, Terry ascribed evil motives to everyone.

The VA diagnosed Terry with Post Traumatic Stress Disorder, which he certainly did have. However, his astute parents felt that something more was happening. They feared for Terry's safety and the safety of others. His paranoia had increased to the point where when he saw someone jogging down his street he was convinced they were scoping out his place and planning on returning later to rob him. He had called the local police so many times that they threatened to arrest him for harassment. It probably didn't help matters that the college students who lived next door to Terry would throw beer cans in his yard at night to intentionally aggravate him. Terry's brain image showed left temporal problems and indeed when we focused his treatment on this area much of his paranoia went away.

The Non-Dominant Temporal Lobe

The right temporal lobe is usually the non-dominant one. Problems in this area of the brain can render a large impact upon someone's social skills. The right temporal lobe interprets what we see and hear in life. It enables us read the emotion in people's faces—discerning if they are happy, sad, bored, or mad. It also helps us decode the intonation in others' voices—to know if they are kidding, being serious, or sarcastic. Problems in this area can lead to misperceiving motives, emotions, and intent.

These people struggle comprehending social cues. Parents often describe these children as "they don't get it." Indeed, many autistic spectrum children will have some amount of dysfunction in the non-dominant temporal lobe.

Kristin has profound deficits in this area. While she can display an outgoing friendly demeanor, she lacks in her ability to discern how she comes across to others and how they come across to her. She will fail to realize that Sue and Jerry are aggravated with her in one setting and then turn around and think they are mad at her for something else when they most surely are not. Numerous times I've attempted joking with Kristin—every once in a while she will crack a smile, but for the most part she takes what I say literally.

There have been numerous cases of right temporal lobe injury causing a phenomenon known as propagnosia—the inability to recognize familiar faces. Even more interesting is that people who have this problem are usually unaware of it.

The right temporal lobe is also believed to be involved in religious experience and to ponder of the meaning of the universe. This is no surprise since this is an area of the brain that tries to interpret life to us. Preoccupation with moral or religious issues can be a factor in right temporal lobe dysfunction. Throughout her life there have been times that Kristin has become engrossed with religious ideation.

Either Temporal Lobe

Some issues such as these can be seen with injury to either or both temporal lobes.

Emotional Stability

The temporal lobes help regulate our emotional control (along with the Deep Limbic System). The diamond shaped amygdala plays an important role in how we react to the world. When it fires appropriately we react to events around us logically in a controlled manner. However, abnormal functioning in this area can render us with unstable reactivity to life's situations-- leading to frequent and intensive mood swings. These people often present complaining of severe moodiness. They may be diagnosed with bipolar spectrum disorders.

Illusions

Most of us are familiar with optical illusions—where you see one object appear bigger than another when they are the same size, or something appears to be moving when it is still. Your mind wrongly interprets what it sees. Illusions can occur with dysfunction of the temporal lobes. The most common ones are:

- Seeing shapes or shadows moving out of the corner of your eyes.
- Seeing objects morph in size and shape. They may even morph into other objects. One patient of mine would frequently see the zebra head that her father had mounted on the wall of their home grow horns. She also witnessed the zebra's face show expression—sometimes it would laugh at her, at other times it frowned or grimaced.
- Hearing a buzzing sound or static when nothing is there.
- Unexplained smells—these are usually unpleasant. One lady could always smell rotting flesh in her house, though no one else could smell it and her house had been searched thoroughly.
- Feeling skin sensations—one patient felt people burning him with cigarettes. Another lady was afraid to sleep at night because she could feel spiders crawling on her though neither she nor anyone else could ever find these spiders.

Seizures

Seizures (multiple episodes are known as epilepsy) can originate in the temporal lobes. These seizures can produce illusions like the ones described above. They can also produce the sensation of déjà vu—the feeling that you've done something or been somewhere before when you haven't, or the opposite jamais vu—a feeling that you've never done something or been somewhere when you indeed have. Feelings of unprovoked fear can also accompany these seizures.

Temporal lobe seizures often consist of a one to two minute episode of loss of awareness with your surroundings. During this time the person may make odd movements, such as smacking their lips and swallowing. They may even get up and walk around like their drunk. I had one patient who pulled a knife on some other shoppers in a home supply store during her seizure episode. There is often confusion after the seizure.

Headaches

Frequent headaches are a common complaint from those with temporal lobe injuries. These headaches can be migraines, coupled with nausea and sensitivity to light, or they might simply be tension headaches. Anticonvulsant medications help regulate temporal lobe activity—this may also help explain why they help relieve migraines and other types of headaches.

The Trifecta

Dysfunction in the non-dominant temporal lobe can result in the misperceiving of social situations and injury to the dominant temporal lobe can then lead to aggressive impulses. Add to this a poor functioning prefrontal cortex, which doesn't shut down impulses and you have the perfect set up for aggression.

For someone with this type of brain injury even driving down the road can be a challenge. Say someone cuts you off in traffic, you might initially sense some anger at being wronged, but then you think, "Well that guy's a jerk who didn't want to wait his turn," and you go on about your business. The person with problems with their temporal and frontal lobes may perceive the situation differently. Adding a little paranoid thinking he may presume that "This guy did this to piss me off!" Now frustrated he feels a surge of aggression towards that person and the thought, "I'll ram his car with mine and show him" occurs. The reasoning of the prefrontal cortex does not kick in and say, "Hang on, this is not a good idea," and in a fit of rage one car slams the other. So something originally very insignificant has now spiraled into a huge ordeal.

Temporal Lobe Functions

- Understanding and processing language
- Consolidating memories (short-to-long term)
- Complex memories
- Retrieving words
- Visual processing and learning
- Reading emotions in facial expressions
- Reading emotion in vocal intonation
- Emotional stability
- Music

Temporal Lobe Problems

- Memory problems, amnesia, interference with long-term memory
- Seizures
- Aggression (temper)
- Misinterpreting social cues
- Sensitivity to slights—paranoia
- Social skill struggles
- Difficulty recognizing facial expression (also in recognizing faces)
- Difficulty decoding vocal intonation
- Dark or violent thoughts
- Emotional instability
- Reading problems
- Word understanding problems (Wernicke's area)
- Auditory processing problems
- Abnormal sensory perceptions (visual and/or audi-

tory distortions)
- Fearfulness (anxiety)
- Frequent déjà vu or jamais vu
- Periods of spaciness or confusion (brain fog)
- Headaches
- Religious or moral preoccupation
- Persistent talking

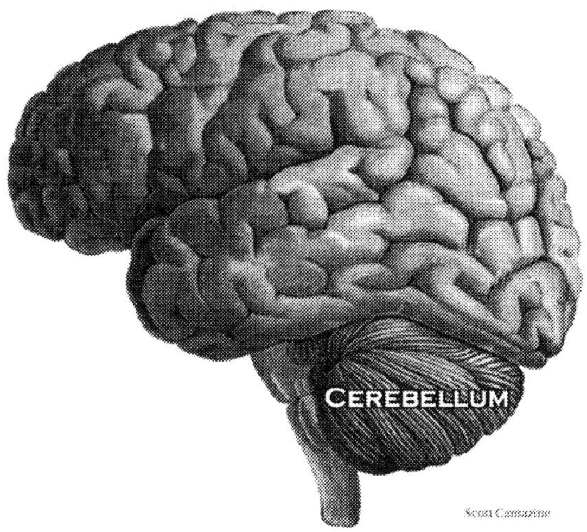

The Cerebellum

The cerebellum is a small structure at the back of our brain. Though it makes up only 10% of the brain in size it contains about one half of the neurons in the brain. This is normally the most active area of the brain and has a large impact on our functioning.

The cerebellum regulates our timing of movements. For instance, when you walk you step forward with your right leg and as soon as it touches the ground your left leg steps forward (and the pattern continues). Your cerebellum oversees the movement of each leg and prepares it in getting ready to step forward. Injury to the cerebellum creates problems with coordination and balance. Damage to this area during the birth process can cause cerebral palsy.

Cerebellar injury can result in problems with slow or slurred speech. Pronouncing words requires the coordination of many muscles. Abnormal eye movements (nystagmus) along with tremors can also occur.

Evidence shows the cerebellum is involved in cognitive functioning (thinking and attention). Many believe that it plays a role in regulating the processing speed of the brain. People with a poor functioning cerebellum exhibit slower thinking. They also have trouble learning new information. Alcohol destroys cerebellar cells. Picturing a "burned out" severe alcoholic with slurred speech who sways and staggers when walking can give you a picture of cerebellar dysfunction.

Cerebellum Functions

- Coordination of voluntary movement
- Balance
- Memory for reflex motor acts
- Speech
- Learning new tasks (conditioned learning)

Cerebellum Problems

- Poor coordination
- Gait problems (loss of ability to walk)
- Inability to grab objects
- Tremors
- Vertigo (dizziness)
- Slurred Speech
- Slowed movements

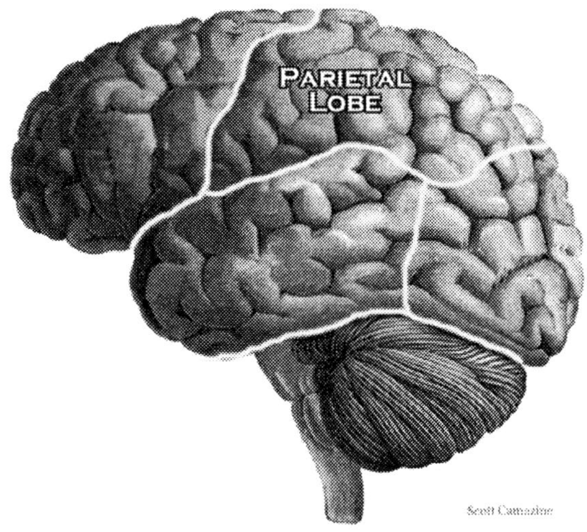

Parietal Lobes

The parietal lobes are located in the upper posterior portion of the brain. They integrate sensory information from the environment. Problems in the parietal lobes can interfere with the ability to regulate sensory input leading to environmental hypersensitivity (light, sound, temperature, and touch).

Parietal dysfunction may cause dysgraphia—a deficiency in the ability to write, dyscalculia—difficulty in comprehending mathematics, and finger agnosia—the inability to distinguish the fingers on the hand. These people may also have trouble with directions, reading maps, and distinguishing their right from their left.

Gary

Gary, a lifelong Floridian, now in his middle forties, decided to nail down the loose shingles on his roof one day during a tropical storm (which shows that his frontal lobes were not working right to start with). He was blown off the ladder as he climbed up to the roof. He sliced a large gash over his right parietal lobe that bled like crazy. The ER doctor stapled it and told Gary to take it easy for the next few days because he might have a mild concussion. Over the next few months his wife, Cheri, noted several changes, but she didn't piece them together until months later in my office.

Gary used to love Cheri's back massages, now he didn't want her touching him at all saying that it felt irritating. Cheri took it as a personal insult and began to wonder if Gary still loved her. The covers on their bed even started to bother him as well as the ceiling fan in their bedroom. Gary claimed that the air blowing on him kept him wide awake the whole night.

Gary called Cheri one afternoon from a gas station near their home asking her to come pick him up. Cheri thought he had car troubles so she went right away. She was surprised upon arriving when Gary told her that he couldn't remember which road he was supposed to turn off on to get into their neighborhood. He finally stopped at the gas station and called after he had driven around for 30 minutes.

Gary's handwriting had changed; it was now much sloppier and difficult to read. Cheri didn't confirm this until she happened to see a letter he had written a few years ago and compared it to his current handwriting. Gary himself even had to admit that there was quite a bit of difference in his penmanship. He had no explanation why.

Gary owned a small printing company with a couple of employees. One of the employees shared his frustration with Cheri that they had recently lost several customers some of them were businesses they had worked with for years. Gary usually took the orders and oversaw the marketing calls. There had been numerous incidents where Gary had forgotten to enter new job orders in the computer. This sort of mistake had been a real rarity in the past. When Cheri approached Gary about it his response was that he may have forgotten an order or two, but definitely not over a dozen as his employees claimed. Somehow Cheri knew the employees were right.

Looking at a SPECT scan of Gary's brain we could see an area of his right parietal lobe that had been injured in his fall from the roof. Cheri, was able to now put together the pieces on his odd behaviors over the last few months. We saw an immediate change in her attitude towards Gary. Now instead of being put out with him, feeling slighted, and that he was antagonizing people on purpose, she realized his actions were largely due to his brain not functioning properly. Cheri then threw her support behind Gary and started working to help him rehab his brain injury.

Cheri came to understand the important fact that people with parietal lobe injuries are often unaware that anything is wrong with them. Gary was not lying when he denied forgetting to enter new job orders into the computer. He wasn't aware of his memory lapses. Woodrow Wilson, who served as the 28th President of our country from 1913-1921, suffered parietal lobe damage from a stroke in 1919. This was hidden from the public and even his cabinet, but advisors (and historians) claim it severely affected his judgment. President Wilson had no insight into the change of his mental capacity and refused to acknowledge that anything was amiss.

Parietal Lobe Functions

- Processing sensory information
- Spatial processing
- Sense of direction

- Reading maps
- Drawing maps
- Distinguishing right from left
- Visual guidance of hands, fingers, eyes, and limbs

Parietal Lobe Problems

- Sensory overload
- Memory
- Seeing moving objects in 3D
- Discerning directions
- Reading a map
- Poor handwriting
- Poor drawing
- Dyscalculia
- Finger agnosia
- Poor awareness of deficits

Occipital Lobe

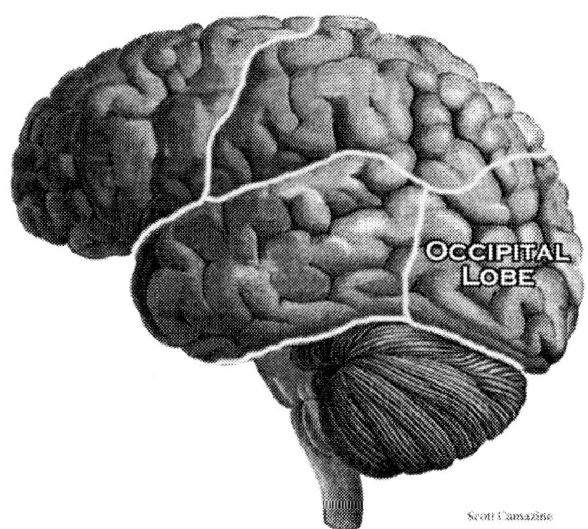

The occipital lobe is the visual processing area of the brain. It is prone to injury due to its location on the surface of the dorsal (rear) of the brain. It is particularly at risk from backwards falls. Damage to this area can result in loss of certain areas of vision (scotomas). Visual illusions and hallucinations may also occur.

Cingulate Gyrus

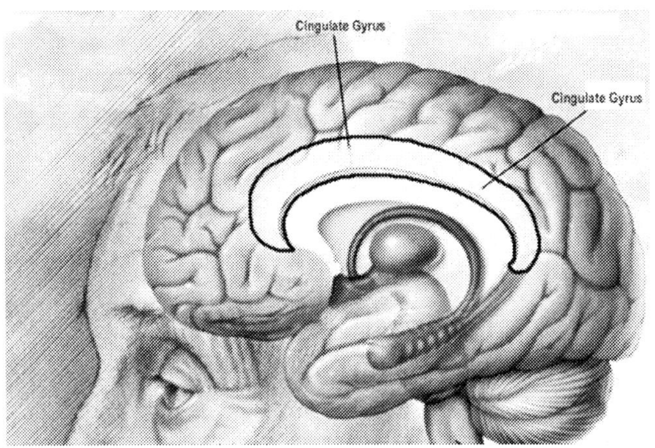

The cingulate gyrus runs right down the middle of the brain from the front to the back. Its location inside the brain, rather than on the surface, offers some protection from injury, but nevertheless the cingulate is often affected—particularly the anterior portion.

The cingulate gyrus has been referred to as the gear shifter of the brain. It allows us to shift attention from subject to subject, see options in situations, and solve complex problems. These abilities are often referred to as "cognitive flexibility." These skills are important in life, especially when it relates to adapting to change, or successfully overcoming challenging obstacles.

People with a healthy cingulate gyrus are able to get along and cooperate with others, be flexible and "roll with the flow." People with problems in this area tend to get stuck on thoughts—thinking the same thoughts again and again and again and again. Their behaviors lean towards the compulsive end. They become very rigid in their dealings with others—difficult to get along with. Some have compared the cingulate gyrus to a caged gerbil that continues in a round and round loop. Here are some other behaviors associated with abnormalities in the functioning of the cingulate gyrus:

Senseless Worrying

If you have a test tomorrow that you have not yet studied for it is a natural and protective response to have some anxiety—hopefully prodding you to study? Worrying however, is (according to the dictionary) tormenting oneself with or suffering from disturbing thoughts. This worrying can escalate to the point of bringing physical or emotional harm to the person. Worrying shuts a person down rather than motivates them to action. It also often accompanies irritability, sleeplessness, and a feeling of hopelessness. Chronic worriers often have over activity in their cingulate gyrus.

Obsessions & Compulsions

When a thought becomes so dominating that we can't turn it off—that's an obsession. This can escalate into a compulsion—a strong irresistible urge to perform an act. The obsession is the thought and the compulsion is the behavior—for instance, an obsessive thought about germs may lead to the compulsive behavior of washing your hands one hundred times a day. Or the thought of becoming fat may become such a preoccupation (the obsession) that you stop eating altogether (the compulsion).

Addictions

Over-activity in the cingulate gyrus can play a prominent role in addiction. Addictions after all, are rooted in some amount of obsessive thought and compulsive behavior. It's easy for those who have never struggled with an addiction to assume that people become and remain addicted because they choose to. Talk to a few people who are dealing with an addiction and they will quickly tell you how much they want to quit, but can't. Their thoughts continue returning to the addiction, which has enslaved them.

Hal's wife, Leslie, reported that his troubles with pornography began after he suffered a head injury. He passed out from a heat stroke while working in his yard one August afternoon. Hal admitted that he used to peek at pornography every once in a while on the internet, but now he couldn't stop himself. He would get up in the middle of the night and go log in to porno sites on his computer—even though he knew full well that Leslie would know what he was doing the next day. Hal's anterior cingulate showed over activity that was off-centered on his brain scan—an indication of injury. When we were able to calm down the hyper cingulate activity he could finally make it through the night without looking at pornography. He was able to shift his mind off of it during the day as well.

Depression

Over-activity in the anterior portion of the cingulate gyrus has been associated with sadness and depression—particularly in one small portion of the cingulate known as Brodmann's Area 25. Serotonin antidepressants have been shown to calm down the activity in this area and thus relieve the depression symptoms. New studies are finding that the antidepressants don't calm the activity down for everyone. There has been quite a bit of success using Deep Brain Stimulation, a treatment for Parkinson's disease to calm down this activity in treatment resistant depression.

Cingulate Gyrus Functions

- Shifting attention from subject to subject
- Adapting to new situations
- Seeing options (cognitive flexibility)
- Moving from idea to idea
- Cooperating with others

Cingulate Gyrus Problems

- Senseless worrying
- Inability to let go of thoughts
- Getting stuck on thoughts (obsessions)
- Getting stuck on certain behaviors (compulsions)
- Inflexible and rigid thinking
- Addictions
- Oppositionality
- Cognitive flexibility
- Obsessive-compulsive disorder
- Eating disorders
- Depression

The Deep Limbic System

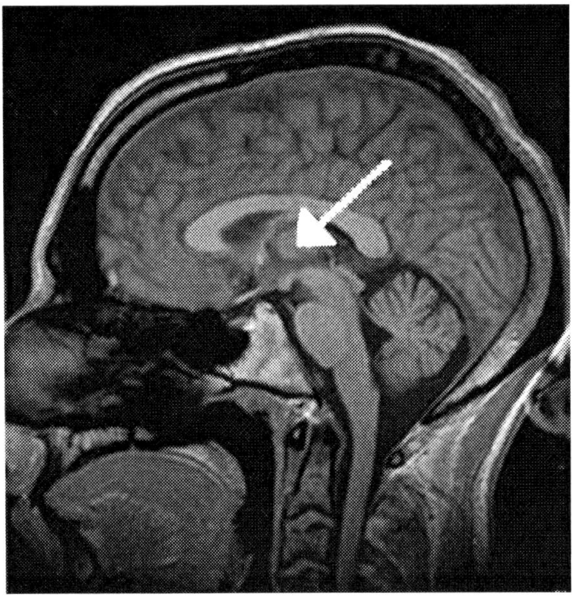

The Deep Limbic System (DLS) lies almost in the center of the brain. It is often referred to as our emotional center. Though not as prone to injury as surface structures of the brain—nevertheless it is often affected by trauma. The DLS maintains intricate connections to many other parts of the brain, especially the Prefrontal Cortex. Thus, injuries sustained to the outer areas of the brain may in turn affect the DLS.

Emotional trauma heavily influences the functioning of the Deep Limbic System. Experiencing a brain injury (and then living with it) is indeed an emotionally traumatic event. It changes everything in life—your thoughts, your feelings, your senses, and your life situation.

The Deep Limbic System activity is often increased in response to emotional stress. An overactive, or inflamed, DLS powerfully affects your moods and emotional sensitivity. Here are some of the functions of the DLS:

Emotional Tagging

Let's say you meet me in my office today for the first time in your life and I'm very friendly, helpful, and encouraging. You'll have good memories of the event and look forward to seeing me again. Say on the other hand I'm extremely rude and I verbally and physically assault you in the meeting—you'll think long and hard before coming to see me again. In fact, you probably won't. Your brain emotionally tags these events.

If the second scenario happened you'd feel anxiety, dread, and fear when someone tried to bring you back to my office. You might feel those same feelings just by crossing paths with a person who looks like me, talks like me, or in some other way reminds your brain of me. Those feelings can overcome you in another office that reminds you of mine. You may find yourself fearful to leave your house and feel more comfortable being alone. You may consciously or subconsciously fear running into me out in public.

Emotional tagging is a protective mechanism needed for our survival. Knowing to steer clear of a dinosaur saved many cavemen's lives. Animals can emotionally tag events too. Now I understand why my dog used to run outside every time my little brother entered the house.

Dysfunction of the Deep Limbic System can hijack the emotional tagging process. It may make us fearful of everyday situations that are indeed safe. I've had patients before that were terrified to leave home. They resisted connecting to others, which bring on a chronic state of loneliness and depression.

The DLS plays a vital role in bonding with people

as well as the ability to give and receive love. It's heavily involved in regulating our libidos. Problems here can lead to an overactive sex drive fueled by lust and passion or no sex drive at all. The DLS is influenced by our reproductive hormones, particularly estrogen and testosterone.

Emotional tagging may be blunted, rather than hypersensitive, leading to a lack of trepidation or concern for circumstances that are dangerous. This is evident with Kristin as she places herself in harm's way over and over, never sensing the gravity of her situation. She doesn't grasp danger on an intellectual level and therefore it doesn't register in an appropriate emotional response.

Mood

Over-activity in the DLS can lead to moodiness, irritability, increased negative thinking, pessimism, and clinical depression. Sometimes though it results in low motivation, and an "I don't care" attitude towards life. However, an inflamed DLS may cause extreme mood swings—tossing that person to ecstatic feelings of euphoria, invincibility, and surging energy, followed by extreme sadness, agitation, despair, to the point of not being able to get out of bed. The swings aren't always this extreme, but do cycle more intensely than normal.

Emotional Regulation

As humans we constantly experience emotions. They can charm us, adding color and spice to life, motivating us to perform good deeds, and to sacrifice for others. Unfortunately, they can also plague us, leading to atrocities like killing, stealing, and cheating. Mentally healthy people are able to balance emotion and reason.

The DLS regulates the emotional gas pedal. Dysfunction on one end results in someone who's emotionally out of control--driven too intensely by their current emotional state. On the other end is someone who's emotionally numb and void. Both sides impair the ability to feel good about yourself, maintain a healthy self-esteem, and function effectively in life. I've seen patients with brain injury flip back and forth from one extreme to the other. The amygdala is an area of the limbic system heavily involved in emotional response.

Richard, and older gentleman, who came in weekly for psychotherapy was an emotional roller coaster, one week he was crying, laughing, and getting so mad in the sessions that he would punch my couch with his fists. The next week his demeanor would be aloof and flat. His mood changes were so prominent that his employer was convinced he was taking drugs and tested him frequently. Richard's family just thought he was crazy and steered clear of him as much as possible. Helping them understand the nature of his deep limbic system and his injury gave them new insight into his strange antics. Their attitude changed from "You're acting this way on purpose and I want to get away from you" to "How can I help you feel better?" Richard gained insight too.

Deep Limbic System dysfunction is often one of the first areas we have to treat on brain injured patients. Getting emotions under proper control is an important step before proceeding further with rehabilitation. Depression can hijack the best of efforts in motivating someone to work hard in rehab. People with brain injuries experience more depression and more suicidal ideation than the normal population. This must be addressed at the beginning of care and through the whole process.

Deep Limbic System Functions

- Regulates the emotional tone of the mind (mood intensity)
- Emotionally tags events
- Stores charged memories
- Modulates motivation
- Influences emotional bonding
- Influences libido

Deep Limbic System Problems

- Mood swings (depression, mania)
- Poor motivation
- Isolation from others
- Irrational anxiety and fear
- Negative emotions
- Inability to feel love
- Feeling emotionally "numb"
- Emotional over reactivity

Chapter 15 Identifying Brain Injuries

Thousands of people suffering from brain injuries are not diagnosed or are misdiagnosed each year in this country. The misdiagnosis may last for years or a lifetime. Everyday victims of brain trauma are repeatedly told they have psychological disorders and are sent to live in psychiatric facilities. Others end up spending years in jail or prison due to their inability to follow the laws of the land. Sadly, many people who cry out that they have a brain injury are accused of feigning their symptoms.

Why do we have such a difficult time recognizing brain injury in our society today? We are living in a time of super advanced technology that can find a virus in the body that's far too small for the human eye to see. We can not only find the virus but type and classify it as well. The brain injured in this country too many times do not receive the attention nor treatment that they deserve. We in the medical community must begin doing a better job of identifying brain injury in our patients. I think there are several reasons we tend to overlook or miss these patients. Here are a few:

People with brain injuries often look normal

If there's a gaping hole in the skull with brains leaking out from a gunshot wound or an automobile crash that's a different story, but most people with brain injuries aren't that obvious. Many of them look just like you and I.

While our skulls are rock hard, our brain tissue is the consistency of soft butter, or tofu (it is not rubbery like people often assume). This puts the brain in a very vulnerable position for injury—especially from bouncing back and forth against the inside of the skull. The brain can be damaged very seriously, yet the skull can be totally intact. Just because the outside of the head looks fine doesn't mean the inside is.

"But Doc, I wasn't knocked out."

How many times have I heard that one as I'm showing a patient his injury on a brain scan? Remember Phineas Gage? He never lost consciousness either. Getting knocked out has to do more with where the injury occurs than how serious it is. An injury in the brain stem will affect consciousness more than one in the frontal lobe. Many physicians still do not realize this. I was recently invited to speak to a brain injury support group and the physician in charge of the meeting, who introduced me to several of the group members, would say things like, "Dr. Clements this is Sharon, she was knocked out for 7 minutes." "This is Harry; he lost consciousness for 30 minutes." Each person in the group rated their severity (like a badge of honor) on how long they had endured unconsciousness. Family members, doctors, and even victims themselves may downplay the notion of a head injury if there was no loss of consciousness.

Sometimes a brain injury can be sustained without your head even making impact. Vehicle accidents can accelerate and decelerate the head very quickly, which causes the brain to bounce off of the inside of the skull. I once saw a lady who sustained a massive brain injury in a car wreck, but her insurance was refusing to take responsibility for any of her medical bills for brain rehab, because the police report stated there was no evidence that the lady's head actually made contact with the windshield of her car. The insurance representative could not comprehend how this lady had a head injury and insinuated she was faking. He did however acknowledge that babies can die from bleeding in the brain in "shaken baby syndrome" even though their heads do not hit anything.

We're not looking

Psychiatrists and neurologists are the two primary medical specialties who treat brain disorders. My specialty—psychiatry—I must ashamedly admit, are the only medical specialists who don't regularly look at the organ we treat. We diagnose brain problems based strictly on symptoms and behaviors. Since many brain injury symptoms overlap with psychiatric disorders like schizophrenia and bipolar, we routinely diagnose those disorders and start treating without looking any further.

Patients like Kristin often start off on one psychiatric medicine and then when the symptoms don't improve we add another, then another, then another. It's not unusual to see a brain injured patient come in on 5 or 6 different medications. If there's no improvement after a while these patients are given a diagnosis of personality disorder, which is basically saying, "It's your own fault you're not getting better, not mine."

Psychiatry is rarely involved with finding the root cause of a problem. We tend to just try to calm the symptoms and then say it's genetic, preferring to blame everything on a "crazy uncle."

Our tests are incomplete

Neurologists are much better when it comes to looking at the brain. CT scans (Computed Tomography) and MRI's (Magnetic Resonance Imaging) are the mainstays in neuroimaging to look at the brain. These scans look at the brain's anatomy. They can identify bleeding, tumors, and even areas of dead and injured tissue in the brain. One problem is that people with mild to moderate brain injuries often have totally normal CT's or MRI's (sometimes they can be normal even in severe injuries). What does the doctor do then?

I've seen hundreds of patients from all types of doctors who are dealing with this very issue. A brain injury is suspected, but the scans are normal. In fact, this happened with Kristin. Some physicians will go on with further testing (which we will talk about in this chapter) others will deem it a behavior or psychiatric problem and refer that patient to the psychiatrist with the medical record signed off saying, "No findings of organic brain damage." Go back to the "We're not looking" section to see what happens then.

Brain-injured people are not good self advocates

This is hardly their fault. Brain-injured people rarely have the insight or capacities to study the internet and medical journals in order to correctly diagnose themselves. Thankfully, Kristin has parents who were able and willing to spend countless hours advocating on her behalf. I've met very few other brain-injured patients who've been this blessed.

A few years ago I recommended to a head-injured patient of mine (from a motorcycle incident) that he apply for disability because of his inability to sustain work. The state insisted that he be evaluated by one of their physicians, which is not unusual. I was surprised when he later came in and brought me his rejection letter. As I was reading over the medical report they stated his main complaints were anxiety and not sleeping well, there was no mention of prior brain injury. The physician obviously didn't read any of the medical report I had sent. When I asked him,

"What did you tell them about your brain injury?" His reply was, "Nothing doc, and I'm really disappointed that she (the state physician) never asked me about it one time." "Why didn't you tell her?" I questioned him. "I don't know," was all he could say.

I've always remembered his situation because it shows how physicians often aren't considering brain injury and patients don't always explain it clearly.

Brain-injured patients are often non-compliant

If your thinking, reasoning, memory, and emotional control are compromised how compliant would you be with following doctors orders and living a healthy lifestyle? People with brain injuries often don't take their medications regularly, especially if they don't understand what their purpose is. They might not even realize that they do need help. Brain-injured people often don't show up to their scheduled doctors' appointments. They may forget they had an appointment, not realize it is important to go, or even be paranoid of physicians.

People with brain injuries frequently have poor diets. This is not surprising in someone with impulse control problems who gets hungry and is surrounded by food. Drug and alcohol abuse is common after a brain injury. Here again, someone with poor impulse control and reasoning skills who is offered drugs will have a strong tendency to take them.

Brain-injured people frequently live life as it comes. Their minds operate in the here and now—not in the future or the past. They may stay up all night then sleep the whole next day. If they want to smoke a cigarette they will likely light one up and never have a thought about lung cancer. These actions may send a message to the doctor that the patient doesn't care about his own life. Sometimes the doctor's attitude can be, *"If they don't care then why should I?"* This is probably done more on a subconscious level that a conscious one. I've learned that when I see this type of behavior that there is probably something more going on with this patient that I haven't discovered yet.

Brain Injury patients are likely to have poor support

Many brain injured patients are estranged from their families. Some choose to walk away from their families, like Kristin did, but in my practice I've seen more experiences where the families distance themselves from the brain injured person. Their inappropriate behaviors are deemed "character" or "moral" weaknesses. Concerned family members will often start out trying to help a brain injured person, but after a while when that person can't hold a job or function in society and refuses to heed the advice of family members the withdrawal of support follows.

Medicare doesn't care.

Many brain-injured patients end up in the Medicare system due to their disabilities. Medicare's goal is not to get you well. It's a huge bureaucracy run by government workers who don't know their constituents. You are simply a number to them. Their goal is to take care of you in the cheapest way possible—so they can make their budgets and keep their jobs. This may mean that you don't get the diagnostic testing that you need to determine a brain injury.

Don't get me wrong there are some very good physicians, nurses, and healthcare professionals working with Medicare patients. They too are very dismayed with the system, but they have been hamstrung and have very little authority or power to change it. If you are in the Medicare system my advice to you is find a good doctor who will advocate strongly for your care.

Patients forget about injuries

I've had patients tell me they never had any type of head injury before and then later call me back and explain how they totally forgot about an injury in their childhood or teen years—sometimes the nature of these injuries were very serious. I've had other people recount episodes where they've hit their head and then gone to the emergency room. They'll say the doctors told me that I was fine and had no injury. Sometimes the extent of the testing done in these instances was merely checking reflexes and pupils. Past injuries can be easy to forget, especially if they weren't deemed serious at the time.

Diagnosing Brain Injuries

As I said earlier, many of us in psychiatry are guilty of failing to thoroughly look for a brain injury before diagnosing someone with a psychiatric condition. The way we diagnose and treat patients here in the 21st century is still quite archaic. I compare what happens in psychiatry to someone who goes to the eye doctor complaining that something is wrong with his vision. The eye doctor goes into a sample closet and pulls out a pair of eyeglasses and has the person wear them for a month and then come back. If their sight is not better then he goes back into a sample closet and brings out another pair for them to try. This continues until finally a pair is found that improve the patient's vision. The treatment then becomes wearing that pair of glasses.

Thankfully, the eye docs I know don't do that. They check you for eye trauma (bleeding, infection, etc…), they check you for stigmatisms, high blood pressure, and other medical problems such as diabetes, which if not corrected will damage your vision. Yes, they may give you a pair of glasses to wear if needed, but not before they search for the underlying causes of your vision problem.

How can we look at the brain? X-rays are too low resolution to tell us much in detail about the brain. They are more or less used to search for skull fractures. CT scans and MRI's are higher resolution and used first line in suspected brain trauma. They are anatomical scans as they evaluate the anatomy, or structure, of your brain.

Functional Brain Imaging

Functional scans measure how your brain is functioning rather than the anatomy. SPECT (Single Photon Emission Computed Tomography) scans, PET (Positron Emission Tomography) scans and fMRI's (functional Magnetic Resonance Imaging) are different types of functional scans. PET scans measure the glucose metabolism in the brain, while SPECT and fMRI measure the blood flow activity. They basically tell us 3 things: which areas of your brain are working well, which areas have too much activity, and which areas have too little activity. Brain injuries will show up in certain patterns. Usually they present as areas of under activity, but they can show over activity.

SPECT and PET Imaging

SPECT and PET scans are nuclear medicine studies. They are performed by injecting a small amount of a radiopharmaceutical (an unstable atom) into the patient's arm. Active brain cells take up the radiopharmaceutical as it breaks down (decays) it emits ultraviolet light, which is detected by the cameras in the scanner. The more active an area of the brain is the brighter it shows up on the scan. Functional scans are much more sensitive when it comes to looking for trauma. Both types of scans give physicians a great view of the brain, inside and out. PET scans are usually more expensive than SPECT scans because they use a radiopharmaceutical that has to be produced on site. SPECT imaging is easier to do on an outpatient basis.

It's not unusual for people with brain trauma to have normal brain structure (anatomy) while their brain functioning is abnormal. Indeed, one of the hallmarks of brain injury is that neurons may not die, but instead undergo chemical changes after an injury that interferes with their functioning. If brain trauma is suspected and CT's or MRI's are normal, your doctor should order a functional scan. Some physicians will even start with a functional scan.

What's the holdup?

If these scans are more sensitive why aren't they used more often? One reason is lack of familiarity. Many physicians had no experience ordering functional brain images in their residency training and just have never done so. Many hospitals are not equipped for functional brain imaging—they may have a SPECT or PET scanner, but it is set up for heart, thyroid, or bone studies. Radiologists on the hospital staff may not have much experience reading these types of brain images, so they have trouble distinguishing what's normal versus what's abnormal.

Insurance companies often won't reimburse hospitals or patients for functional scans—even though they would greatly help clarify the diagnosis and likely save the insurance companies money in the long run. Hopefully, as doctors continue learning more about this technology and advocating better for it, the insurance companies with modify their policies on denying proper medical care for their constituents.

Other studies:

Neuropsychological testing

Neuropsychological testing is not a direct measurement of the brain itself, but rather tests cognitive skills, such as attention, learning, and memory—and looks for impairments of skills. Specific neurological tests have been designed that are known to be linked to particular brain structures or pathway. How the person performs on these tests is usually compared to a group of people similar in age, education and even ethnicity.

Neuropsychological testing was used extensively before brain imaging emerged to locate the area of the brain that was injured. Today it is very useful to evaluate the extent of the effect a brain injury has caused. Neuropsychological testing can also be performed periodically to measure the progression of improving brain function. It's a tremendously useful tool.

Electroencephalogram (EEG)

An EEG measures the electrical activity produced by the brain. This is recorded from electrodes placed on the scalp. EEG's are routinely used to locate areas of the brain that may be causing seizures. In hospital settings it is also used to verify brain death (no electrical activity). Areas of injured brain can also show abnormal electrical activity. EEG's give valuable information about the activity on the surface of the brain, which is great in identifying brain injuries. They can't give much information though about what's happening deep in the brain.

The Fallout of Brain Injury

Sadly, many people with brain injuries today are living in the streets of our cities, our jails, or locked up in psychiatric facilities. Many of these people who were once productive and full of life are now hopeless and just going through the motions of living. Too many times the end result is wasted resources and wasted lives.

Drugs & Brains

Alcohol and drug use puts a person at higher risk for a brain injury. The opposite is also true—brain injury puts a person at higher risk for alcohol and drug abuse. This is particularly true with a frontal lobe injury where reasoning skills along with impulse control is affected. These people are often unable to grasp a clear understanding of choices and consequences. They live in the here and now. The problem with this type of thinking is when someone offers you drugs your immediate thought is, "Hey, this will make me feel better." You're not concerned with what will happen when it wears off or what kind of trouble you could get into, or that it could kill you. You're not even worried that you're spending your last amount of money to acquire these drugs—you'll worry about that later.

Alcohol and drugs worsen brain functioning even further. Not to mention they take someone who has poor reasoning and impulse control and lower those skills even more. I've witnessed on numerous accounts marijuana make someone with a brain injury extremely paranoid. I've also witnessed brain injured people drink themselves into a stupor with alcohol. They have no idea how to pace themselves or drink socially, basically they drink till they run out or pass out, whichever comes first.

Drugs are probably the single most issue that causes strife between the brain injured and their families. Many times families will blame that person's problems on the drug use. They see the root of the problem as one of a character deficiency. It's easy to make people with impaired reasoning skills buy into this as well. Family members and friends can see the damage that the drugs are doing and are shocked and dismayed that the user can't see the effects or is oblivious to them.

Randy, a young man who suffered an undiagnosed brain injury in a rugby game during his junior year of college, experienced a pretty radical personality transformation. Quiet and shy in the past he became loud and obnoxious. He rarely drank before his junior year, but started getting sloshed at the rugby parties after the game. He received 2 DUI's, had to go to the hospital once for alcohol poisoning, wrecked his car into the side wall of the dorm, and got put on probation at school for pulling his pants down in the lobby of the ladies dormitory (that's a whole other story) before his parents had to intervene.

Randy's parents blamed much of his behavior on hanging around with the rugby team and minimized any effect a brain injury might have had until another doctor pointed out to them that Randy had hung out with the rugby team since his freshman year and had never acted like this. Several of Randy's friends on the rugby team reported that he was like a wild man at the parties and would be intoxicated to the point where he couldn't walk usually after only an hour or so. On numerous occasions they pleaded with him to stop drinking and would take away his keys. They were frightened by the change in his behavior.

Kristin lacks reasoning skills when it comes to drugs and alcohol. This is one of her biggest obstacles to living independently. Drugs and alcohol are practically everywhere in our country. If she was on her own she would take whatever pill, joint, or drink is offered to her without realizing anything is wrong with that. She probably doesn't even put it together that drinking alcohol will make her drunk.

Future Dementia

Brain injury increases the chances of developing Alzheimer's disease down the road—this risk can be increased up to five fold. Alzheimer's involves the progressive break down of functioning in the temporal, parietal, and frontal lobes. We now know that genetics are one of the fundamental components in deciding who will develop Alzheimer's. Recent estimates suggest that 1 out of 2 people in this country over the age of 85 are struggling with dementia. The thought is that if you live long enough you will be touched by it. Prior brain trauma can definitely bring the symptoms of dementia on earlier.

We do have treatments for dementia, but they basically only slow its progression. This is a huge area of pharmaceutical research with dozens of prospective cognitive enhancing agents currently undergoing clinical trials. The hope is that in the next decade a safe medication can be found that will reverse the effects of dementia; right now though our hope is in recognizing dementia early. Treating dementia is similar to cancer—the earlier you find it the better the outcome is. This is why it is important to recognize brain injuries and monitor these people closely for any signs of encroaching dementia.

Brain Healing

One of the most important aspects of identifying brain injury is that it allows us to begin rehabilitating that injury. The predominant thought until the mid 1990's was that the brain cannot repair. I remember being told as a teenager that drinking a shot glass full of whiskey on an empty stomach killed around 20 thousand brain cells (that's why I always drank on a full stomach). Well, you might not get those exact neurons back, but we do know now that the brain can and does heal itself. Two main ways this healing occurs are from the growth of new neurons (neurogenesis) and the growth of existing neurons.

It's mind boggling when you consider just how we change as human beings. Old cells are constantly dying and new ones forming. Your bone marrow makes over 2 million new cells each minute! Seven years from now your human body will consist of almost entirely different cells than it does today—yet, you will still be you. Your brain is included in this as well. The normal functioning brain loses an estimated 30,000 brain cells per day, that's almost 1 every 3 seconds. However, a healthy brain will be able to replace that amount of lost cells. As you age though, the balance starts tipping and more neurons are lost than replaced. This is why brain atrophy (shrinking) is a normal occurrence with age. The point where the balance tips is believed to be somewhere around 40 years of age in normal individuals. Unhealthy living, a brain insult, psychiatric problems, too much stress, poor diet, and taking the wrong medications are some of the factors that can tip this balance earlier. The good news is that with changes, this lost ground can often be made up.

Our brains release BDNF (brain derived neurotrophic factor), which is a type of nerve growth factor that supports the survival of existing neurons and encourages the growth of new neurons. Molecular neuroscientist, Dr. John Medina, refers to BDNF as

"Miracle Grow" for the brain. We don't understand completely yet how this process works, but there is evidence that physical exercise spurs the release of BDNF and that high levels of cortisol (the body's stress hormone) impedes the release of BDNF. Mice that are born without the ability to make BDNF die soon after birth, therefore we know that BDNF is required to help surviving neurons function. As we continue learning more about BDNF and its role we will be better able to treat brain injury in the future.

New neurons do not mature fast; in fact, it takes years. A mature neuron can connect with over 40 thousand other neurons. These connections require time, learning, and effort. As you learn and face new consequences in life your neurons make new connections. If you started learning to play a musical instrument or a foreign language tomorrow, new connections (or tracks) would be laid between neurons. Your brain is also constantly pruning connections.

Brain injury results in the death of neurons. Other neurons don't die, but they are incapacitated and don't work right due to chemical changes that occur. When this happens, the surrounding neurons can branch out and establish new connections. In this manner they can learn to take over the functions of the dead or damaged neurons. Here again, this process is not completely understood.

Take for instance a lady who has a stroke and loses functioning of the right side of her body. She often goes to rehab after release from the hospital. Over time she slowly gains back some use of that right side. It's rarely ever as good as before. There are many factors that help determine the degree of recovery. The point is this—the brain is able to repair itself through new neurons and new connections.

Chapter 16 Treating Brain Injuries

Yes, there is good news—the brain can heal! Here's more good news—we can treat brain injuries. Proper treatment of brain injuries can help aid in the healing process, it can help abnormal functioning areas of the brain work more properly, and it can improve the cognitive and emotional problems that result from these injuries.

I hope to explain some of the process that happens to brain cells after an injury without getting too technical here. The focus of this book is Kristin's story with some education about brain injury. This is not an exhaustive work on brain biology and physiology, so please realize that I'm tremendously oversimplifying this.

I stated earlier that neurons are connected to each other—well they're not actually physically connected. Small spaces called synaptic gaps remain between the axons and dendrites.

Synaptic Gap

Neurons communicate with each other through these gaps by releasing neurotransmitters. One neuron releases the neurotransmitter which is collected in receptors by a receiving neuron. It is actually electrical impulses (called action potentials) in a neuron that prompts it to fire (release its neurotransmitter(s)). This process repeats itself down the line as one firing neuron spurs others to fire.

Neurons fire when their electrical charge inside the cell reaches a certain voltage. Neurons must maintain a certain electrical charge to function properly. It's just like your computer which won't work right unless is has a proper amount of electricity (too much makes it surge and too little makes it drag).

Electrolytes (ions) are particles with an electrical charge that are constantly moving in and out of the brain cells. Some are positively charged (cations) such as potassium (k^+), sodium (Na^+), and calcium (Ca^{++}), and others carry a negative charge (anions), such as chlorine (Cl^-) and phosphorous (P^-). Injury to a neuron affects its ability to maintain its proper range of electric charge—usually by altering its ability in regulating the flow of ions in and out of the cell. Much of this process we don't understand very well yet. This is sometimes referred to as secondary injury—the neuron doesn't die from being stretched or shaken, but it doesn't work right afterwards.

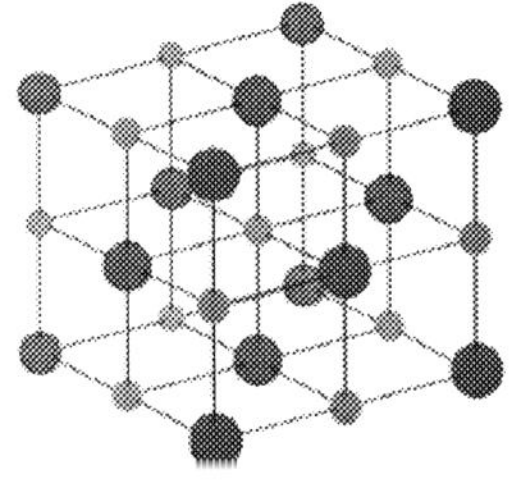

Ions

It's easy to think that an area of brain injury by nature will be underactive, but that's not necessarily true. Areas of dead tissue will be underactive, but injured neurons may be underactive or hyperactive. Losing the ability to regulate electrolyte flow can affect activity in either direction. Medications work by increasing brain activity (excitatory) or calming it down (inhibitory). One example is anti-seizure medications; a seizure starts when a small area of the brain is excessively firing and that spreads to a wider area of the brain—a generalized seizure spreads across the whole brain. Anti-seizure medications calm down those areas of excessive firing by decreasing the electrical voltage—this is done by letting more Cl^- into the cell or keeping more Ca^{++} out.

If a cell fires too much, it can die from overexcitation. There is evidence that this is one of the processes happening in Alzheimer's disease. This is also one of the ways that alcohol and drugs kill brain cells. It's very important to keep your brain cells as healthy as possible.

Brain Injury Rehabilitation

Brain rehab consists of using the proper nutrients, supplements, and medications (if needed) to help maintain a good activity level. This helps both the current functioning and healing of the brain. The other imperative component is providing an atmosphere of learning and training that helps the brain rewire.

The brain's electrical activity works in circuits. As neurons learn to fire in certain circuits those connections pathways are strengthened and thus learning occurs. Say you take up learning a foreign language tomorrow; you'll struggle with each new word you learn. Every time you read or try to pronounce that word neurons fire in a certain path (now remember I'm simplifying this). As you practice pronouncing it more, that sequence of certain neurons fires together more and the circuit gets ingrained. The saying among brain scientists is that neurons that fire together—wire together. Pretty soon saying and reading the word comes easy—you hardly have to think about it—that circuit is established. The circuit will weaken over time if you stopped learning the foreign language—that's why we forget 90% of the stuff we learn in school (about 99% of algebra).

Neuron injury disrupts brain circuitry. People may have to relearn lifelong acquired skills, such as reading, writing, speaking, or even recognizing faces. One aspect of brain injuries is that two people can receive a similar trauma to a similar area of the head and present with quite different symptoms—much depends on what circuits are damaged.

Just like physical rehab rebuilds your muscles after an illness or accident, brain rehabilitation rebuilds your brain circuitry. Relearning does occur. Damaged neurons can survive if their cell bodies remain intact. They can re-grow dendrites and refine connections with surrounding neurons. Nearby neurons compensate by growing new dendrites and making new connections as well. The older you are though, the slower this growth occurs.

Every day counts.

One of the main concerns with Kristin, along with scores of other brain-injured people, is that they're not getting the care they need. Each day they sit in jail, a psychiatric ward, or a boarding home, they're losing the chance to retrain their brain. It's not the fault of the facility; those places were created to serve different purposes.

It's extremely important to perform thorough cognitive and occupational testing on anyone suspected of brain injury. The deficits can sometimes be sneaky. I treated Lana, whose husband Keith was hit in the head by a falling brick on a construction job. When Keith began experiencing headaches and memory lapses a few months later, Lana convinced him to see his physician and tell him about the incident. Keith returned home saying the doctor told him that if his problems just developed they couldn't be from an incident that was months ago (Lana didn't accompany him to the doctor visit, so we'll never know exactly what was said).

A week later Keith stayed home alone one Saturday while Lana visited her parents. Returning home that evening she found the fire department converged on her house. Tragedy had struck. Keith's body was found in the attic where he had suffocated from smoke inhalation from a fire that had started on the stove where he was cooking. Why he was in the attic no one knows to this day.

Looking back Lana can see how Keith's thinking had changed his ability to perform tasks, as well as his memory. She feels remorse over his death and that perhaps she could have done more to find out what was going on in his brain. A nursing friend of hers had suggested that Keith have some neuropsychiatric testing done, but Lana wasn't aware of how that could help.

Good rehabs start with testing skills—and retesting them frequently to monitor progress. How well a person can read and follow directions, cook a meal, make decisions, manage a checkbook, live on a budget, drive a car, communicate their wants, and make emotional connections to others determines their future treatment and recovery.

It's a family affair.

Parents, spouses, children and other close family members should be included in the rehabilitation process. A brain injury affects the whole family and rarely is anyone prepared to deal with the consequences. Counseling and education for the spouse is a must! I've seen too many marriages end in divorce after head trauma. The spouse often doesn't understand how to deal with this partner who now has different thoughts, feelings, and behaviors. Some brain injuries bring about a whole personality change, which changes the whole paradigm of the marriage.

Wives may have to become the primary financial provider for the family. One lady, whose husband could no longer practice law after a brain injury in an automobile accident, enrolled in law school and went to work for her husband's former law firm a few years later.

Intimacy, romance, and sex will change (and not necessarily for the worst). Brain injuries change temperaments—temporal lobe injuries can result in a mild-mannered husband who now exhibits a ferocious temper. Frontal lobe injuries can turn the most empathic thoughtful wife into an impulsive shopper who drains the family savings. The number of different changes that occur in people after a brain injury can be mind boggling.

Children need to learn that when someone hurts his brain, he will act differently. The children of one of my patients were distraught when they saw their father, who returned from Iraq with a brain injury; kill the family dog in a fit of rage. They were so fearful that their mother had to send them to live with her parents for the summer while their father recuperated. No one had explained to them that their father had been hit in the head and his personality may be a little different. They spent that summer in counseling and learned that their father was not an evil animal torturer who would possibly harm them next. Their father received the help he needed as well.

When children and adolescents suffer brain trauma it changes the whole dynamics of the family. Parents often have to learn how to reassess their expectations of that child. I've seen cases where college students are now reverted back to a child's state of mind. Parents have to learn how much responsibility and freedom to afford the teenager who sustains an injury. As a youth minister in my 20's, I remember, Valerie, a high school junior who almost died from a horrible car accident. I didn't know much at all about brain injury then, but I do remember her parents struggling to decide if she was ready to start dating again. Did she have the emotional capacity? Did she have enough reasoning to keep her from being taken advantage of? Could she control the sexual impulses of a 17 year old girl? (All parents may ask that question though.)

Valerie's little sisters had to come to grips that now they were the big sisters in every circumstance but age. Valerie's friends had to get to re-know her. This process was awkward and stressful for Valerie's family and friends. Valerie did well and today she's married with children of her own.

I remember her father telling me that all they thought about after the accident was her living and being able to walk and talk. They never considered that Valerie might be able to walk and talk, but have a different personality. They assumed if she made it she would be the same old Valerie they knew before, but she wasn't. Interestingly though, there were many things about the new Valerie that they enjoyed. Her sisters claimed that she was frequently uptight, bossy and stingy before the accident, but now she giggled a lot, didn't worry about things, and let them borrow her clothes anytime they wanted.

Drugs and Brains don't mix.

Alcohol and illegal drugs cause brain damage every bit as real as brain trauma. (For the sake of brevity I will refer to both of them as simply drugs from here forward.) Rather than a localized area of damage as in some cases of brain trauma, drugs usually exert their toxic effects on the brain globally. Drugs kill brain cells by overstimulation (excitotoxicity), by interrupting their blood supply (damaging the capillaries that feed them), and cutting off oxygen to cells (anoxia).

Brain injury and drug abuse is often a double whammy. Drug abuse damages brains and brain injured people are more at risk to abuse drugs, thus adding more insult to their brain. Drugs can be tempting in this group for several reasons. People with prefrontal cortex injury may be very impulsive and live totally in the current moment; Kristin is a good example of this. She does not realize or even concern herself with the consequences that her drug use will bring.

Drugs may temporarily relieve emotional suffering. Smoking marijuana often calms down anxiety and fear in those with an overactive cingulate gyrus or basal ganglia. They often say it allows them to rest their brain and feel "normal" for a while. Of course, as soon as the drug wears off they go right back to the previous state. Sometimes the anxiety and fear will be worse than it was before using. The bad part is that the only way these people know how to stop that rebound anxiety is to use again. It doesn't take too long before they can't function without drugs in their system and life revolves around obtaining that substance.

Drugs may also temporarily help patients function better. Someone with a prefrontal cortex injury may be more focused, motivated, and less impulsive after using cocaine. Here again, that only lasts a few hours until the effects of the drug wear off. Drugs don't impart a lasting change. While they may be of some benefit in the short-term the end result is that they inhibit your brain from healing, inflict more damage on it, harm your physical health, and eat up much precious time and resources. Another sad fact is that many brain-injured people are doing time in the penal system today for drug crimes. This again delays their ability to get the help they need.

Some substance abuse rehabs programs offer good cognitive retraining. They understand that drugs wreak havoc in the brain and their patients' brains need re-wiring. For people with brain injuries who are also battling substance abuse, the best starting place is probably in a full-time substance abuse program. (Watching "Celebrity Rehab with Dr. Drew" does not qualify for rehab).

The down side

Unfortunately, the bad news that I alluded to earlier—thousands of brain injured people across this country today aren't getting the help they need—has become a desperate situation. Multiple factors play a part in the inadequate care of the brain injured—here are some of the most prominent ones:

Lack of awareness

Many healthcare professionals still have 20th century mentalities, saying that there is nothing that can be done for a brain injury. This type of mindset naturally leads to the conclusion of, "Why look if nothing can be done?"

Lack of adequate testing

Many medical facilities don't have the capacity to perform functional brain studies. They may have a SPECT, PET, or fMRI scanner, but it's often not set up for brain imaging. CT scans and MRI's are great studies, but they look at the anatomy. Not assessing the brain's functioning will result in missing many injuries.

Lack of integrated healthcare

Most patients and physicians will agree that our healthcare system needs to be revamped. The leading healthcare system in the world has succumbed to being dominated by bureaucrats from managed care and insurance companies. This change has disintegrated and fragmented healthcare. (I'm not blaming them for this happening—the blame rests squarely with me, a physician, and my medical colleagues, for allowing people without medical training to take over our profession.)

Insurance companies are good at what they do—making a profit. The problem is that profiting is more important than the well-being of their constituents. Insurance companies limit what medical tests and procedures they will allow patients to receive. These companies employ people with very little educational training or medical knowledge to make medical decisions. Physicians are often hassled if they object to or appeal the decisions of the insurance companies on behalf of their patients.

I still vividly recall speaking with a female a few years ago who represented a large insurance company in California. I needed to have some labs approved for a patient. When the girl found out that I lived in Newport Beach she excitedly shared with me how she had just been there a few months earlier with some girlfriends celebrating her graduation from high school. She then proceeded to tell me how she got so drunk she passed out and then woke up on the beach the next morning with no pants on. I was embarrassed and wondered what this had to do with my patient's request for services. She then told me that she didn't think my patient really needed those tests, but since I had been so nice she was going to allow it this time. The basis of her decision told me how subjective and flawed the health insurance system is.

Hopefully physicians and patients will say enough is enough and reform the healthcare system. Then patients can choose to go to the doctors who give them the best care as opposed to who their insurance tells them they have to see. And we are allowed to put patient care first.

Lack of time with patients

The prominence of managed care and the proliferation of medical malpractice lawyers over the last few decades have created an insurmountable amount of paperwork for healthcare providers. We spend a large part of our day filling out meaningless forms that are read by few and stored away in files for years. Physicians have to see more patients today as well; so, busy work plus more patient visits means less face time for each patient. This doesn't allow us to know many of our patients as well as we need to. Hopefully this changes.

What's coming?

Exciting new treatments are just down the road. We're learning improved techniques in saving the lives of those with acute severe brain trauma. One reason we're seeing so many soldiers come back from Iraq with head trauma is due to advanced in medicine. In wars past these soldiers would have died on foreign soil.

Brain imaging techniques are improving. We're learning more information about what we're seeing as our experience grows. Scans also teach us on how our treatments are working. We're learning what effects different meds, supplements, and cognitive therapies have on restoring brain function. New scanning techniques, such as magnoencephalography (MEG) are developing. MEG measures magnetic forces emitted by neurons and can detect changing activity in a neuron with millisecond resolution.

We're learning more about trophic factors—molecules found in the brain that are involved in the healthy development and survival of specific groups of neurons. Discovering the ability to reproduce these factors will greatly advance the treatment of many types of brain disorders. Researchers have already found value in one of these factors—Nerve Growth Factor (NGF). When infused into the brain of aged rats with memory deficiencies these rates were able to learn and remember tasks as well as healthy rats their age.

Injecting stem cells into areas of damaged brain tissue is a hope on the horizon. A large percentage of neurons function as support cells—they surround, protect, and nourish axons—allowing them to conduct their signals efficiently. Stem cells look promising in reproducing these types of cells.

Future gene therapies will focus on inserting healthy genetic material into the brain. For example, someone who suffers from severe depression may benefit from receiving cells with genes programmed to make the neurotransmitter serotonin.

What can I do today?

Let your voice be heard! Tens of thousands of people who suffer a brain injury this year will not get diagnosed. Even more will not get sufficient treatment. There are untold numbers who already have brain injuries that are missing out on compassionate care—they're called crazy, mentally challenged, weak, moral failures, fakers, whiners, head jobs, a brick shy of a load, and those who "just don't get it." These people may be your family members, your neighbors, your friends, or perhaps even yourself. We must be the voice for these people or they will continue to waste life away in the back wards of obscure chronic psychiatric facilities. They will remain lonesome, scared, and confused night after night, week after week locked up in our prisons.

We can help give these brothers and sisters better lives—the chance to be healthy, happy, and productive—especially if we raise our voices together!

The Epilogue

California, 2009

We continue to fight the battle to have Kristin and millions like her recognized as brain-injured. Every year in the United States 1.3 million suffer a traumatic brain injury. Thousands of America's soldiers are coming back from Iraq and Afghanistan with more than injured limbs and emotions...they are coming back with brain injuries. Traumatic brain injury has been called the "signature wound" of the Iraq war. These wounded warriors deserve a functional brain scan using the latest technology. With a PET, fMRI or SPECT scan they can get the accurate diagnosis and help that their bravery merits. Their families who sacrificed so much must not live with the wicked stew of confusion that spiraled around our family. You can join us. The time is urgent for our voices to be heard.

The battle to put traumatic brain injury into public focus will not be easy. We can testify to that. After special witnesses like a psychiatrist, a neurologist and a gynecologist testified before an administrative judge, our lawyer led the Orange County Regional Center on a clear summary of our daughter's disability before the age of 18. After days of courtroom experience to fight for our daughter's care, we were once again turned down from receiving assistance. The current system is strong and unwilling to bend easily and is nearly bankrupt. Meanwhile, the need for brain injury care continues to grow. Who will be a voice for those who cannot think for themselves?

We have registered a non-profit 501c3 organization called B.R.A.I.N. and an acronym meaning Brain

Rehabilitation And Injury Network. We are moving forward to build a long-term living campus for those eighteen years of age and older who have a brain injury and who need short-term rewards, unconditional love, engaging social atmospheres, challenging cognitive therapy, exercise, art, music appreciation, work skills and much more. We envision a place where we will provide a healthy and happy lifestyle opportunity for those who have had to fight to survive. Please visit www.thebrainsite.org to see how you can help.

I've told you our story about our dear Kristin, and how her story has enveloped us. What is your story? Contact me at sue@thebrainsite.org and tell me how brain injury has affected you and your family. I understand. I care. We can work together to make this life full of positive purpose for our loved ones.

This book is dedicated to Kristin…

Our precious daughter, sister, enigma, heartache and hero. Your hidden brain injury made us a mystery to you and you to us. Yet one thing that was never uncertain to any of us was our love for you. Your injury has taken us all to a place where we have learned how to love without conditions. God is still writing our story of courage, understanding, love and generosity. We will always be together.

Mom, Dad, Jon and Jana